DAVID BUSCH'S
COMPACT FIELD GUIDE
FOR THE

NIKON®
D5500

David D. Busch

David Busch's Compact Field Guide for the Nikon® D5500
David D. Busch

Project Manager: Jenny Davidson

Series Technical Editor: Michael D. Sullivan

Layout: Bill Hartman

Cover Design: Mike Tanamachi

Indexer: Valerie Haynes Perry

Proofreader: Mike Beady

ISBN: 978-1-68198-042-3

1st Edition (1st printing, November 2015)

© 2016 David D. Busch

All images © David D. Busch unless otherwise noted

Rocky Nook Inc.

802 E. Cota Street, 3rd Floor

Santa Barbara, CA 93103

USA

www.rockynook.com

Distributed in the U.S. by Ingram Publisher Services

Distributed in the UK and Europe by Publishers Group UK

Library of Congress Control Number: 2015952002

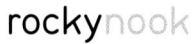

Contents

About the Author

With more than two million books in print, **David D. Busch** is the world's #1 selling digital camera guide author, and the originator of popular digital photography series like *David Busch's Pro Secrets, David Busch's Quick Snap Guides,* and *David Busch's Guides to Digital SLR Photography.* As a roving photojournalist for more than 20 years, he illustrated his books, magazine articles, and newspaper reports with award-winning images. Busch operated his own commercial studio, suffocated in formal dress while shooting weddings, and shot sports for a daily newspaper and an upstate New York college. His photos and articles have appeared in *Popular Photography, Rangefinder, Professional Photographer*, and hundreds of other publications. He's also reviewed dozens of digital cameras for CNet and other CBS Interactive publications, and his advice has been featured on NPR's *All Tech Considered*. Visit his website at www.nikonguides.com.

Introduction

Throw away your cheat sheets and command cards! Are you tired of squinting at tiny color-coded tables on fold-out camera cards? Do you wish you had the most essential information extracted from my comprehensive *David Busch's Nikon D5500 Guide to Digital SLR Photography* in a size you could tuck away in your camera bag? I've condensed the basic material you need in this handy reference book, *David Busch's Compact Field Guide for the Nikon D5500.* In it, you'll find the explanations of *why* to use each setting and option—information that is missing from the cheat sheets and the book packaged with the camera. You *won't* find the generic information that pads out the other compact guides. If you found this ready reference useful, I think you'll want to have my full-sized guide, too. This one will help you set up and use your Nikon D5500, and the other is an in-depth guide to explore as you master the full range of things this great camera can do.

Chapter 1

Quick Setup Guide

This chapter contains the essential information you need to get your Nikon D5500 prepped and ready to go. You'll learn how to use a few of the basic controls and features, and how to transfer your photos to your computer. If you want a more complete map of the functions of your camera, skip ahead to Chapter 2. Live view is touched on only briefly in this chapter; if you want to begin using live view or shoot movies immediately, check out Chapter 6.

Pre-Flight Checklist

The initial setup of your Nikon D5500 is fast and easy. You just need to learn a few controls, charge the battery, attach a lens, and insert a memory card.

Charging the Battery

When the EN-EL14a battery is inserted into the MH-24 charger properly (it's impossible to insert it incorrectly), an orange Charge light begins flashing, and remains flashing until the status lamp glows steadily, indicating that charging is finished, generally within about 90 minutes. When the battery is charged, slide the latch on the bottom of the camera and ease the battery in, as shown in Figure 1.1.

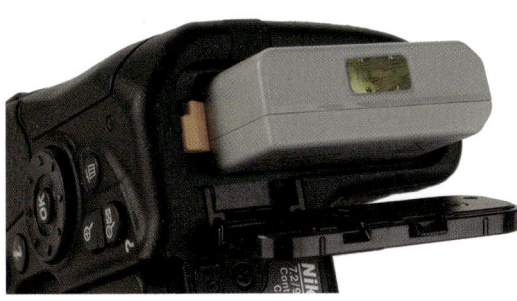

Figure 1.1
Insert the battery in the camera; it only fits one way.

Introducing the Basic Controls

You'll find descriptions of most of the controls used with the Nikon D5500 in Chapter 2, which provides a complete "roadmap" of the camera's buttons and dials and switches. However, you may need to perform a few tasks during this initial setup process, and most of them will require the MENU button, the multi selector pad, and command dial. Figure 1.2 shows the location of these controls.

- **MENU button.** It's located to the left of the LCD monitor. When you want to access a menu, press it. To exit most menus, press it again.
- **Multi selector pad.** This is a thumbpad-sized button with projections at the up, down, left, and right "navigational" positions, plus a button in the center marked "OK." With the D5500, the multi selector is used exclusively for navigation; for example, to navigate among menus on the LCD monitor or to choose one of the 39 focus points, to advance or reverse display of a series of images during picture review, or to change the kind of photo information displayed on the screen. The OK button is used to confirm your choices.
- **Command dial.** This dial, located on the right corner of the top surface, is used for some navigation and to make settings, such as f/stop or shutter speed.
- **Touch screen.** You can use your fingers to tap, slide, pinch, and stretch on the D5500's LCD monitor. I'll show you how to use these gestures next.

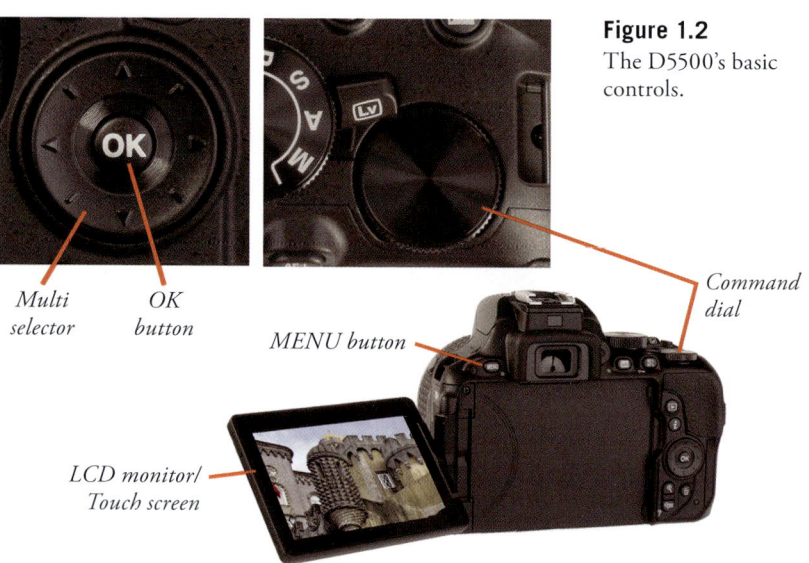

Figure 1.2
The D5500's basic controls.

Multi selector   *OK button*   *MENU button*   *Command dial*

LCD monitor/ Touch screen

The Touch Screen

The LCD monitor supports a limited number of touch operations, such as adjusting some camera settings, zooming in and out of the image in playback, and, in live view only, selecting a focus point and taking a picture by tapping the screen. When adjustments are available, a white rectangle is drawn around the indicator that can be accessed by touch. You will see up/down and left/right triangles used to adjust increments, or a reversed arrow that represents "return" to the previous menu. Available gestures include:

- **Tap.** Touch the screen with a single finger to make an adjustment. For example, you can tap an up/down or left/right triangle to increment or decrement a setting, such as monitor brightness. In live view, when Touch Shutter is activated, tapping the screen locates the focus point at the tapped location and takes a picture. When Touch Shutter is deactivated, tapping the screen simply relocates the focus point. (You'll find a Touch Shutter on/off icon at the left side of the live view screen, as explained in Chapter 6.)

- **Flick.** Move a single finger a short distance from side to side across the monitor. Note that if a second finger or other object is also touching the monitor, it may not respond. During playback, a flick to the right or left advances to the next or previous image.

- **Slide.** Move a single finger across the screen in left, right, up, or down directions. You can use this gesture during playback to scroll around within a zoomed image.

- **Stretch/pinch.** Spread apart two fingers to zoom into an image during playback, or pinch them together to zoom out.

A TOUCH OF SCREEN

Throughout this book, when telling you how to use a menu or feature, I'm going to stick to referring to the physical buttons and dials rather than explicitly say something like "press OK or tap the Return icon on the LCD monitor." Nikon really needs to redesign the camera interface to take full advantage of the touch screen capabilities. Cameras from other vendors, for example, use slider controls instead of left/right touch arrows to make many adjustments. While some may find Nikon's implementation helpful, it's really best when used with the Touch Shutter feature in live view, zooming in/out of a playback image, or, perhaps, tapping a menu entry rather than scrolling up/down with the directional buttons.

Because the screen uses static electricity, it may not respond when touched with gloved hands, fingernails, or when covered with a protective film. I have a "skin" over my D5500's monitor and it works just fine; your experience may vary, depending on the covering you use. Don't use a stylus, pen, or sharp object instead of a finger; if your fingers are too large, stick to the physical controls such as the buttons or dials. As you'll learn in Chapter 4, you can enable or disable the touch controls or enable them only during playback, using an option in the Setup menu.

Setting the Clock

The in-camera clock might have been set for you by someone checking out your camera prior to delivery. Press the MENU button to the left of the viewfinder, and then use the multi selector to scroll down to the Setup menu (it's marked with a wrench icon), press the multi selector button to the right, and then press the down button to scroll down to Time Zone and Date, and press the right button again. The options for setting the 24-hour clock will appear on the screen that appears next. They include Time Zone, actual Date and Time, Date Format, and Daylight Saving Time (on/off).

Mounting the Lens

If your D5500 has no lens attached, you'll need to mount one before shooting:

1. Select the lens and loosen (but do not remove) the rear lens cap.
2. Remove the body cap on the camera by rotating the cap away from the shutter release button.
3. Once the body cap has been removed, remove the rear lens cap from the lens, set it aside, and then mount the lens on the camera by matching the alignment indicator on the lens barrel with the white bump on the camera's lens mount (see Figure 1.3). Rotate the lens toward the shutter release until it seats securely.
4. Set the focus mode switch on the lens to AF or M/A (Autofocus with manual adjustment possible). If the lens hood is bayoneted on the lens in the reversed position, twist it off and remount with the "petals" (if present) facing outward. A lens hood protects the front of the lens from accidental bumps, and reduces flare caused by extraneous light arriving at the front of the lens from outside the picture area.

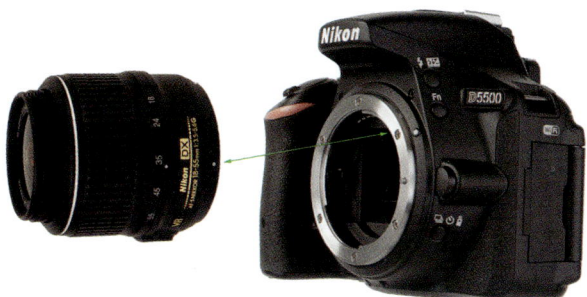

Figure 1.3
Match the indicator on the lens with the white dot on the camera mount to properly align the lens with the bayonet mount.

Adjusting Diopter Correction

If you are a glasses wearer and want to use the D5500 without your glasses, or to add further correction, you can take advantage of the camera's built-in diopter adjustment, which can be varied from –1.7 to +0.5 correction. Press the shutter release halfway to illuminate the indicators in the viewfinder, then move the diopter adjustment control next to the viewfinder (see Figure 1.4) while looking through the viewfinder until the indicators appear sharp. Should the available correction be insufficient, Nikon offers nine different Diopter-Adjustment Viewfinder Correction lenses for the viewfinder window, ranging from –3 to +1, at a cost of $16 to $20 each.

Diopter adjustment control

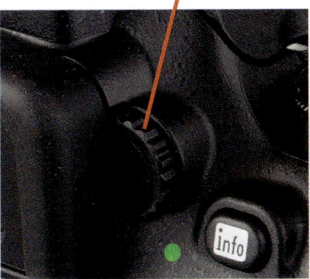

Figure 1.4 Viewfinder diopter correction from –1.7 to +0.5 can be dialed in.

Inserting and Formatting a Memory Card

Next, insert a memory card. Slide the cover on the right side of the camera toward the back, and then open it. Inside, you'll find an SD card slot. You should only remove the memory card when the camera is switched off, or, at the very least, when the yellow-green card access light (just above the Trash button on the back of the camera) that indicates the D5500 is writing to the card is not illuminated.

Insert the memory card with the label facing the back of the camera, oriented so the edge with the gold connectors goes into the slot first (see Figure 1.5). Close the door, and, if this is your first use of the card, format it (described next). When you want to remove the memory card later, press the card inward, and it will pop right out.

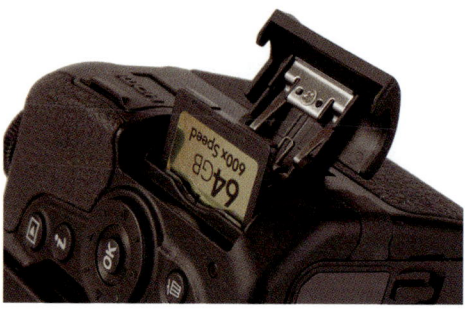

Figure 1.5
The memory card is inserted with the label facing the back of the camera.

I recommend formatting the memory card before each shooting session, to ensure that the card has a fresh file system, and doesn't have stray files left over. Format *only* when you've transferred all the images to your computer, of course.

- **Setup menu format.** Press the MENU button, use the up/down buttons of the multi selector (that thumb-pad-sized control to the right of the LCD monitor) to choose the Setup menu (which is represented by a wrench icon), navigate to the Format Memory Card entry with the right button of the multi selector, and select Yes from the screen that appears. Press OK to begin the format process.

Selecting an Exposure Mode

The Nikon D5500 has four types of shooting modes: advanced modes/exposure modes; auto modes, which includes Auto and Auto (Flash Off); and a third set, which Nikon labels Scene modes. Also available is a fourth option, Special Effects, which allows you to process your images with some retouching effects, such as Color Sketch or Miniature Effect, as the picture is actually taken. Nikon D5500 has two types of exposure modes: Auto/Scene/Effects modes, in which the camera makes virtually all the shooting decisions for you, and advanced modes, which include semi-automatic and manual exposure modes (Program, Shutter-priority, Aperture-priority, and Manual).

Choosing a Scene Mode

The two Auto modes and 16 Scene modes can be selected by rotating the mode dial on the top right of the Nikon D5500. The Auto and Auto (Flash Off) settings have their own positions on the dial, while the Scene modes can be selected by rotating the mode dial to the SCENE position, and then rotating the main command dial to select one of the additional modes.

These options include:

- **Auto.** In this mode, the D5500 makes all the exposure decisions for you, and will pop up the internal flash if necessary under low-light conditions. The camera automatically focuses on the subject closest to the camera (unless you've set the lens to manual focus), and the autofocus-assist illuminator lamp on the front of the camera will light up to help the camera focus in low-light conditions.

- **Auto (Flash Off).** Identical to Auto mode, except that the flash will not pop up under any circumstances. You'd want to use this in a museum, during religious ceremonies, concerts, or any environment where flash is forbidden or distracting.

- **Portrait.** Use this mode when you're taking a portrait of a subject standing relatively close to the camera and want to de-emphasize the background, maximize sharpness, and produce flattering skin tones. The built-in flash will pop up if needed.

- **Landscape.** Select this mode when you want extra sharpness and rich colors of distant scenes. The built-in flash and AF-assist illuminator are disabled.

- **Child.** Use this mode to accentuate the vivid colors often found in children's clothing, and to render skin tones with a soft, natural-looking texture. The D5500 focuses on the closest subject to the camera. The built-in flash will pop up if needed.

- **Sports.** Use this mode to freeze fast-moving subjects. The D5500 selects a fast shutter speed to stop action, and focuses continuously on the center focus point while you have the shutter release button pressed halfway. However, you can select one of the other two focus points to the left or right of the center by pressing the multi selector left/right buttons. The built-in electronic flash and focus assist illuminator lamp are disabled.

- **Close Up.** This mode is helpful when you are shooting close-up pictures of a subject from about one foot away or less, such as flowers, bugs, and small items. The D5500 focuses on the closest subject in the center of the frame, but you can use the multi selector right and left buttons to focus on a different point. Use a tripod in this mode, as exposures may be long enough to cause blurring from camera movement. The built-in flash will pop up if needed.

- **Night Portrait.** Choose this mode when you want to illuminate a subject in the foreground with flash (it will pop up automatically, if needed), but still allow the background to be exposed properly by the available light.

The camera focuses on the closest main subject. Be prepared to use a tripod or a vibration-resistant lens like the 18-55 VR kit lens to reduce the effects of camera shake.

- **Night Landscape.** Mount your camera on a tripod and use this mode for longer exposure times to produce images with more natural colors and reduced visual noise in scenes with street lights or neon signs.
- **Party/Indoor.** For indoor scenes with typical background lighting.
- **Beach/Snow.** Useful for bright high-contrast scenes with sand or snow. The built-in flash and AF-assist lamp are disabled.
- **Sunset.** Emphasizes the rich colors at sunset or sunrise, disables the flash, and may use a slow shutter speed, so consider working with a tripod.
- **Dusk/Dawn.** Similar to Sunset mode, but preserves the subtle colors in the sky just after sunset, or just prior to dawn.
- **Pet Portrait.** An "action" mode specifically for fast-moving, erratic subjects, such as pets.
- **Candlelight.** Disables your flash to allow photographs by candle; a tripod is recommended.
- **Blossom.** Uses a small f/stop to expand depth-of-field when shooting landscapes with broad expanses of blossoms. This Scene mode may result in longer shutter speeds, so consider using a tripod.
- **Autumn Colors.** Makes reds and yellows in Fall foliage richer.
- **Food.** Boosts saturation to make food look more appetizing in your snaps.

Special Effects modes, available when you rotate the mode dial to Effects, provide additional special looks. Of the following, Color Sketch, Miniature Effect, and Selective Color are available in both still and live view/movie-shooting modes.

- **Night Vision.** Produces images of the darkest scenes using the D5500's high ISO sensitivity settings. Use a tripod, because blur is likely with the longer shutter speeds. Under this dim lighting, you'll need to focus manually if working with the optical viewfinder; autofocus is available only in live view.
- **Super Vivid.** Provides brilliant, rich, contrasty colors.
- **Pop.** Increased saturation without excessive contrast.
- **Photo Illustration.** Sharpens the outlines and reduces the number of colors to create a posterization effect.
- **Toy Camera Effect.** Blurry, vignetted pictures that look as if they were taken with a toy camera. In live view, you can vary the strength of the effect.

- **Miniature Effect.** This effect is widely becoming known as "Tilt/Shift" because it can be reproduced with special lenses that tilt and shift the plane of focus. By throwing backgrounds and foregrounds out of focus, the subjects in the middle of the frame appear to be miniatures photographed with shallow depth-of-field. A cool effect, but it's already starting to be over-used.

- **Selective Color.** You choose the colors that you want to dominate the main subject in your image, and everything else is rendered in black-and-white.

- **Silhouette.** Exposes for bright backgrounds, turning foreground objects into underexposed silhouettes.

- **High Key.** Exposes for bright scenes with lots of highlight areas.

- **Low Key.** Tailors exposure for darker scenes, retaining murky shadows while allowing highlights to remain.

Choosing an Advanced Mode

The advanced modes include Programmed auto (or Program mode), Shutter-priority, Aperture-priority, and Manual exposure mode, known collectively as PSAM modes, for their initials. These are the modes that allow you to specify how the camera chooses its settings when making an exposure for greater creative control. Figure 1.6 shows the position of the modes described next.

- **P (Program).** This mode allows the D5500 to select the basic exposure settings, but you can still override the camera's choices to fine-tune your image, while maintaining metered exposure.

- **S (Shutter-priority).** This mode is useful when you want to use a particular shutter speed to stop action or produce creative blur effects. Choose your preferred shutter speed, and the D5500 will select the appropriate f/stop for you.

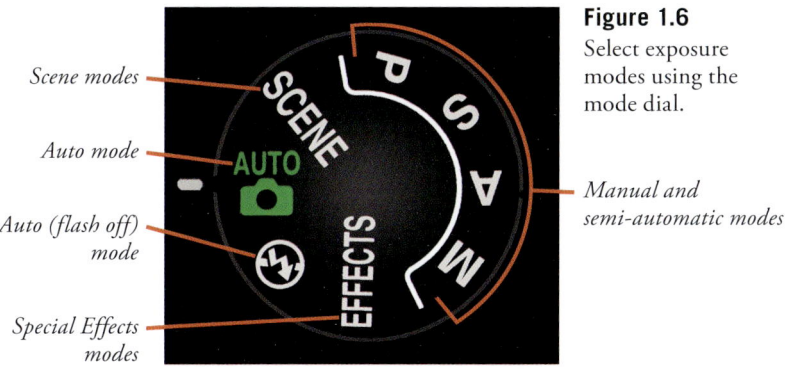

Scene modes

Auto mode

Auto (flash off) mode

Special Effects modes

Figure 1.6
Select exposure modes using the mode dial.

Manual and semi-automatic modes

- **A (Aperture-priority).** Choose when you want to use a particular lens opening, especially to control sharpness or how much of your image is in focus. Specify the f/stop you want, and the D5500 will select the appropriate shutter speed for you.

- **M (Manual).** Select when you want full control over the shutter speed and lens opening, either for creative effects or because you are using a studio flash or other flash unit not compatible with the D5500's automatic flash metering.

Changing Settings with the Information Edit Screen

All the settings that follow can be changed using the information edit screen. You can see your current settings from the shooting setting screen, shown at left in Figure 1.7. If this screen is not shown on the LCD monitor, you can produce it by pressing the Info button located to the right of the viewfinder window. You can change any of the settings arrayed along the bottom two rows of the shooting setting screen. To do so, press the *i* button, positioned next to the multi selector at roughly the 11 o'clock position. That summons the *information edit* screen (at right in the figure), which allows you to use the multi selector buttons to navigate to the settings in the bottom two rows. Navigate to the setting you want to change, press the OK button to view your options, and highlight your choice with the up/down multi selector buttons, and press OK again to confirm.

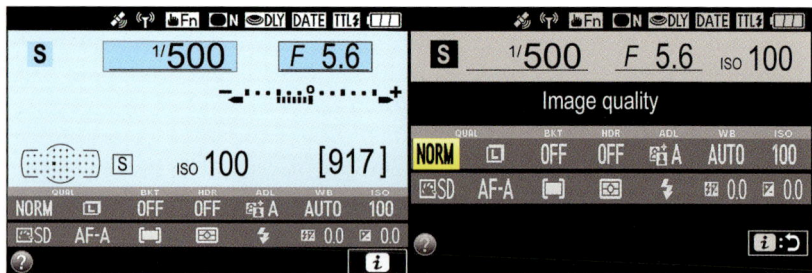

Figure 1.7 The shooting settings (left) and information edit (right) screens.

> **TIP**
>
> The Info button does nothing but switch the display on or off; the *i* button accesses the information edit screen and several other adjustment screens.

Choosing a Release Mode

The release mode determines when (and how often) the D5500 makes an exposure. Your D5500 has seven release (shooting/drive) modes: single frame, continuous L (3 frames per second), continuous H (5 frames per second), self-timer, delayed remote (ML-L3), quick response remote (ML-L3), and quiet shutter release. Change them by pressing the release mode/drive button located on the front of the camera below the lens release button on the left side of the lens mount when you're holding the camera. Hold it down and rotate the command dial to select the mode you want. Press OK to confirm. The release modes are as follows:

- **Single frame.** In this mode, the D5500 takes one picture each time you press the shutter release button down all the way. If you press the shutter and nothing happens (which is very frustrating!), you may be using a focus mode that requires sharp focus to be achieved before a picture can be taken. This is called focus priority, and is discussed in more detail in Chapter 4.

- **Continuous L/Continuous H.** These modes fire off shots at up to 3 or 5 frames per second, respectively. The frame rate can slow down as your D5500's memory buffer fills, which forces the camera to wait until some of the pictures you have already taken are written to the memory card, freeing up more space in the buffer.

- **Quiet shutter release.** This setting, represented by a Q symbol, activates the D5500's "quiet mode," which silences the camera's beep noise during autofocus, reduces the sound the mirror makes when it flips back down, and delays that "noise" until you release the shutter button.

- **Self-timer.** You can use the self-timer as a replacement for a remote release, to reduce the effects of camera/user shake when the D5500 is mounted on a tripod or, say, set on a firm surface, or when you want to get in the picture yourself. Use Custom Setting c3 to specify delays of 2, 5, 10, or 20 seconds. You can also specify the number of shots taken at the end of the elapsed period, and the interval between those shots. Any time you use the camera on a tripod (with the self-timer or otherwise), make sure there is no bright light shining on the viewfinder window; if so, cover it or locate a DK-5 eyepiece cap and block the window.

■ **Delayed remote/Quick response remote.** No special setting of the release mode is necessary when you plug the wired MC-DC2 remote into the side of the camera. However, if you want to use the ML-L3 infrared remote, you'll need to change the release mode to either of these two settings: delayed remote (shutter releases two seconds after you press the button on the ML-L3 IR remote) or quick response remote (the shutter trips immediately when the button is pressed). Once you've selected either of these two release modes, the camera then "looks" for the remote signal for a period of time you specify using Custom Setting c4 (select from 1, 5, 10, or 15 minutes, as described in Chapter 4). As with the self-timer, make sure there is no bright light shining on the viewfinder window; if so, cover it or locate a DK-5 eyepiece cap and block the window.

Choosing a Metering Mode

The metering mode you select determines how the D5500 calculates exposure. Use the information edit screen to change the metering mode. When using any PSAM mode, press the *i* button, navigate the screen to Metering Mode (it's fourth from the left in the bottom row) with the directional buttons, press OK, and then use the left/right directional buttons to select one of the following metering modes: (See Figure 1.8.)

■ **Matrix metering.** The standard metering mode; the D5500 attempts to intelligently classify your image and choose the best exposure based on readings from a 2,016-segment color CCD sensor that interprets light reaching the viewfinder using a database of hundreds of thousands of patterns.

■ **Center-weighted metering.** The D5500 meters the entire scene, but gives the most emphasis to the central area of the frame, measuring about 8mm.

■ **Spot metering.** Exposure is calculated from a smaller 3.5mm central spot, about 2.5 percent of the image area.

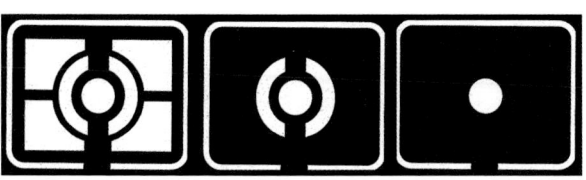

Figure 1.8
Metering mode icons are (left to right): Matrix, Center-weighted, Spot.

Choosing a Focus Mode

You can easily switch between automatic and manual focus by moving the AF/MF, A/M, or M-AF/MF switch on the lens mounted on your camera. You can also select the autofocus mode (*when* the D5500 measures and locks in focus) and autofocus pattern (*which* of the 39 available autofocus points or zones are used to interpret correct focus).

When you are using Program, Aperture-priority, Shutter-priority, or Manual exposure mode, you can select the Autofocus mode *when* the D5500 measures and locks in focus prior to pressing the shutter release down all the way and taking the picture. Choose focus mode by pressing the *i* button and navigating to the second icon from the left on the bottom row of the information edit screen.

The four focus modes when not using live view are as follows (there are additional autofocus modes, when shooting in Live View mode, as I'll explain in Chapter 6).

- **(AF-S) Single-servo autofocus.** This mode, sometimes called *single autofocus*, or AF-S, locks in a focus point when the shutter button is pressed down halfway, and the focus confirmation light glows at bottom left in the viewfinder. The focus will remain locked until you release the button or take the picture. This mode is best when your subject is relatively motionless.

- **(AF-C) Continuous-servo autofocus.** This mode, sometimes called *continuous autofocus*, or AF-C, sets focus when you partially depress the shutter button (or other autofocus activation button), but continues to monitor the frame and refocuses if the camera or subject is moved. This is a useful mode for photographing sports and moving subjects.

- **(AF-A) Automatic autofocus.** In this mode, the D5500 will select from AF-S or AF-C, depending on whether your subject is stationary or moving.

- **(M) Manual focus.** When focus is set to manual by setting the AF/MF switch on the lens, you always focus manually using the focus ring on the lens. The focus confirmation indicator in the viewfinder provides an indicator when correct focus is achieved.

In Live View mode, your focus options, as explained in Chapter 6, are as follows:

- **AF-S.** This single autofocus mode, which Nikon calls single-servo AF, locks focus when the shutter release is pressed halfway. By default this mode uses focus-priority.

- **AF-F.** This mode is roughly the equivalent of AF-C. Nikon calls it full-time servo AF. The D5500 focuses and refocuses continually as you shoot stills in live view or record movies. Unlike AF-C, this mode also uses focus-priority.
- **MF.** Manual focus. You focus the image by rotating the focus ring on the camera.

Choosing an AF-Area Mode

Use the information edit screen, described earlier, to navigate to the AF-area mode entry, the third icon from the left on the bottom row. Your choices are as follows:

- **Single-point.** The camera focuses on a point you select, using the multi selector directional buttons. The focus zones are shown in Figure 1.9. (Available in AF-S, AF-C, and AF-A modes.)
- **Dynamic-area AF (9 points).** You select the focus point, and the camera also uses information from surrounding AF points (nine points, total) to calculate focus. (Available in AF-C and AF-A modes only.)
- **Dynamic-area AF (21 points).** You select the focus point, and the camera also uses information from surrounding AF points (21 points, total) to calculate focus. (Available in AF-C and AF-A modes only.)
- **Dynamic-area AF (39 points).** You select the focus point, and the camera also uses information from surrounding AF points (39 points, total) to calculate focus. (Available in AF-C and AF-A modes only.)
- **3D tracking.** You select the focus point, and the camera will track your subject, using any of the other focus points, as needed, when using AF-A and AF-C modes. (In AF-S mode, focus tracking is not used, as focus is locked in when you press the shutter release halfway.) (Available in AF-C and AF-A modes only.)
- **Auto-area AF.** The D5500 chooses a focus point. (Available in AF-S, AF-C, and AF-A modes.)

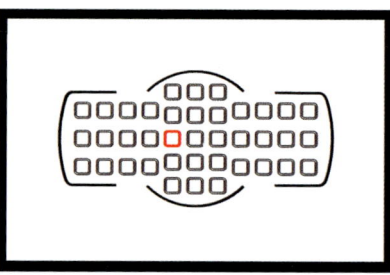

Figure 1.9
The D5500 has 39 focus zones.

Adjusting ISO

If you like, you can custom-tailor your ISO (sensitivity) settings. To start out, it's best to set ISO to ISO 200 for daylight photos, and ISO 400 for pictures in dimmer light. You can adjust ISO now with the information edit screen.

Reviewing the Images You've Taken

The Nikon D5500 has a broad range of playback and image review options. (See Figure 1.10.)

- **View image.** Press the Playback button (marked with a white right-pointing triangle) located just to the right of the LCD monitor above the multi selector to display the most recent image on the LCD monitor.

- **View additional images.** Press the multi selector button left or right or rotate the command dial to review additional images. Press/rotate right to advance to the next image, or left to go back to a previous image.

- **Change information display.** Press the multi selector button up or down to change among overlays of basic image information or detailed shooting information.

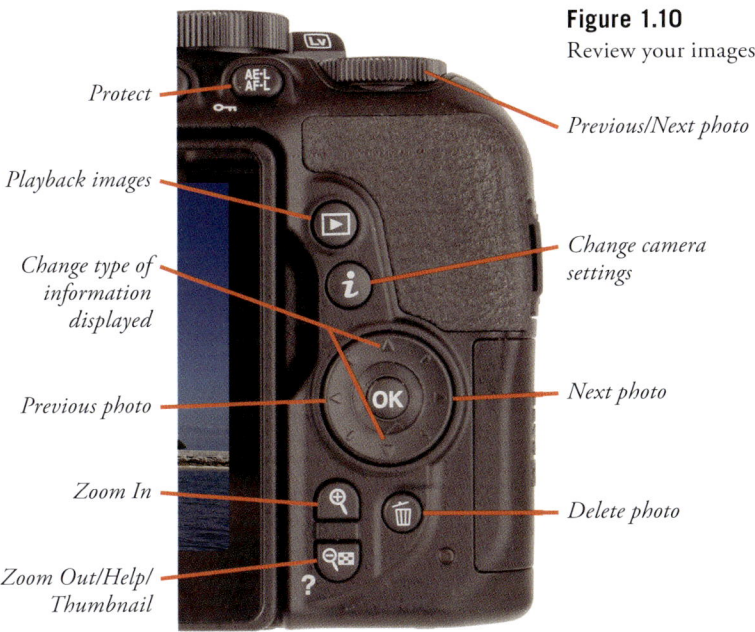

Figure 1.10
Review your images.

Protect

Previous/Next photo

Playback images

Change type of information displayed

Change camera settings

Previous photo

Next photo

Zoom In

Delete photo

Zoom Out/Help/ Thumbnail

■ **Change magnification.** Press the Zoom In button repeatedly to zoom in on the image displayed; the Zoom Out button reduces the image and displays thumbnails and calendar mode. When the image is zoomed in, a thumbnail representation of the whole image appears in the lower-right corner with a yellow rectangle showing the relative level of zoom. At intermediate zoom positions, the yellow rectangle can be moved around within the frame using the multi selector.

■ **Exit image review.** Press the Playback button again, or just tap the shutter release button to exit playback view.

Using the Built-in Flash

The built-in flash is easy enough to work with that you can begin using it right away, either to provide the main lighting of a scene or as supplementary illumination to fill in the shadows. External flash will be covered in Chapter 5.

■ **Activating flash in Scene modes:** The built-in flash will pop up automatically as required in Auto, Portrait, Child, Close Up, Night Portrait, Party/Indoor, and Pets Portrait Scene modes, as well as Color Sketch and Toy Camera Special Effects modes.

■ **Activating flash in advanced modes:** To use the built-in flash in Manual, Aperture-priority, Shutter-priority, or Program modes, just press the flash pop-up button (shown in Figure 1.11). When the flash is fully charged, a lightning bolt symbol will flash at the right side of the viewfinder display.

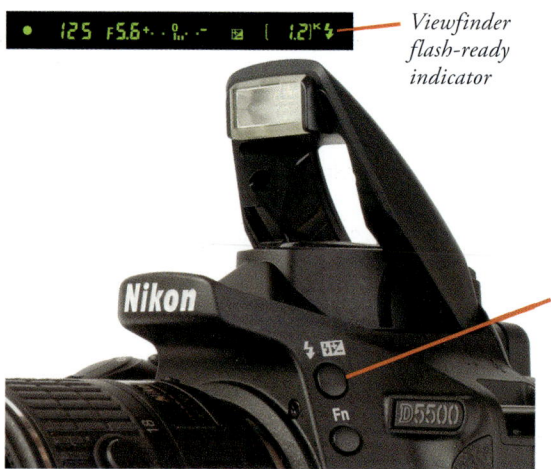

Viewfinder flash-ready indicator

Flash pop-up/ Flash mode/ Flash compensation button

Figure 1.11
The pop-up electronic flash can be used as the main light source or for supplemental illumination.

■ **In P and A modes:** When using P (Program) and A (Aperture-priority) exposure modes, the D5500 will select a shutter speed for you automatically from the range 1/200th to 1/60th seconds. You can select an aperture, and the flash exposure will be calculated automatically.

■ **In S (Shutter-priority) mode:** You select the shutter speed from 1/200th to 30 seconds, and the flash exposure will be calculated automatically.

■ **In M (Manual) mode:** You select the shutter speed from 1/200th (the highest shutter speed that can be used in standard flash modes) to 30 seconds, and aperture. The flash exposure will be calculated automatically.

Transferring Photos to Your Computer

The final step in your picture-taking session will be to transfer the photos you've taken to your computer for printing, further review, or image editing. Your D5500 allows you to print directly to PictBridge-compatible printers and to create print orders right in the camera, plus you can select which images to transfer to your computer.

I recommend using a card reader attached to your computer to transfer files, because that process is generally a lot faster and doesn't drain the D5500's battery. However, you can also use a cable for direct transfer, which may be your only option when you have the cable and a computer, but no card reader (perhaps you're using the computer of a friend or colleague, or at an Internet café).

To transfer images from the camera to a Mac or PC computer using the USB cable:

1. Turn off the camera.
2. Pry back the cover that protects the D5500's USB port, and plug the supplied USB cable into the USB port. (See Figure 1.12.)
3. Connect the other end of the USB cable to a USB port on your computer.
4. Turn the camera on. The operating system itself, or installed software such as Nikon Transfer or Adobe Photoshop Elements Transfer, usually detects the camera and offers to copy or move the pictures. Or, the camera appears on your desktop as a mass storage device, enabling you to drag and drop the files to your computer.

USB port

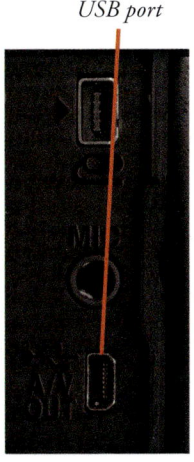

Figure 1.12
Images can be transferred to your computer using an optional USB cable plugged into this port.

To transfer images from a memory card to the computer using a card reader, do the following:

1. Turn off the camera.
2. Slide open the memory card door and remove the SD card.
3. Insert the memory card into your computer's memory card reader. Your installed software detects the files on the card and offers to transfer them. The card can also appear as a mass storage device on your desktop, which you can open and then drag and drop the files to your computer.

Resetting the Nikon D5500

If you want to change from the factory default values, you might think that it would be a good idea to make sure that the Nikon D5500 is set to the factory defaults in the first place. After all, even a brand-new camera might have had its settings changed at the retailer, or during a demo. Unfortunately, Nikon doesn't make it easy to reset *all* settings in the camera to their factory defaults. In fact, there are no fewer than *four* different ways to "reset" the D5500, each of which does slightly different things. Those ways include:

■ **Two-button reset.** This type of "rebooting" changes ten of the most basic settings in your camera, and is useful when you want to cancel the most common changes you make when adjusting your camera. It does not affect all Shooting menu settings, or any of the Custom Setting memory banks, described next. I'll show you how to perform the two-button reset shortly.

■ **Shooting menu bank reset.** The Shooting menu has a separate Reset Shooting menu option that zeroes out the changes you've made to the default options.

■ **Custom Setting menu bank reset.** The Custom Setting menu also has a separate Reset Custom Settings option that zeroes out most of the changes you've made to the default options. A two-button reset does not affect any of the settings in the Custom Setting menu banks.

■ **Cold reset.** The only way to reset *all* of the D5500's internal settings is to remove the battery and allow the internal backup battery to run down until the settings are lost, which can take several weeks or longer. You can remove the battery and then turn on the camera briefly to reset *most* settings, but this won't zero out all settings to the factory defaults as long as some juice remains in the backup battery (which is tucked deep inside the camera and not user-accessible). You might want to try a cold reset if your camera is hopelessly locked up, and you'd like to make one last attempt at restoring it to factory operation before sending it in for service.

Two-Button Reset

Just follow these steps to perform a two-button reset of the camera:

1. **Find reset buttons.** Locate the MENU and Info buttons on the back of the camera to the left and right of the viewfinder window, each marked with an adjacent green dot.

2. **Start reset.** Press and hold the two buttons for more than two seconds.

3. **Release the two buttons.** Your camera's settings have been returned to the factory default.

SHOOTING MOVIES

You'll learn more about shooting high-definition movie clips with your D5500 later in Chapter 6. But if you want to get started right away, it's easy. Just select Live View mode by rotating the spring-loaded Live View (Lv) switch located next to the mode dial on the top right of the camera. When you want to start shooting, press the Movie button, with the red dot in the middle, located on top of the camera, southwest of the shutter release button. Press the Movie button again to stop shooting. Swivel the Lv switch once more to exit live view. That's it!

Chapter 2

Nikon D5500 Roadmap

You should find this roadmap of the functions of the D5500's controls more useful than the tiny black-and-white drawings in the manual packed with the camera, which has dozens of cross-references that send you on an information scavenger hunt through dozens of pages. Everything you need to know about the controls themselves is here. You'll find descriptions of menus and settings in Chapters 3 and 4.

Nikon D5500: Front View

Figure 2.1 shows a front view of the Nikon D5500 from a 45-degree angle. The main components you need to know about are as follows:

- **Shutter release.** Angled on top of the hand grip is the shutter release button, which has multiple functions. Press this button down halfway to lock exposure and focus. Press it down all the way to actually take a photo or sequence of photos if you've changed to continuous shooting modes, or if you've redefined the behavior of the self-timer to take 1 to 9 exposures when its delay has expired. Tapping the shutter button when the D5500's exposure meters have turned themselves off reactivates them, and a tap can be used to remove the display of a menu or image from the rear color LCD monitor.

- **On/Off switch.** Rotating this switch to the detent turns the camera on.

- **AF-assist illuminator/Red-eye reduction/Self-timer lamp.** This LED (not shown in this view; it resides on the front of the camera just below the mode dial) provides a blip of light shortly before a flash exposure to cause the subjects' pupils to close down, reducing the effect of red-eye reflections off their retinas. When using the self-timer, this lamp also flashes to mark the countdown until the photo is taken. It can also illuminate to provide assistance for the D5500's autofocus mechanism at fairly close distances.

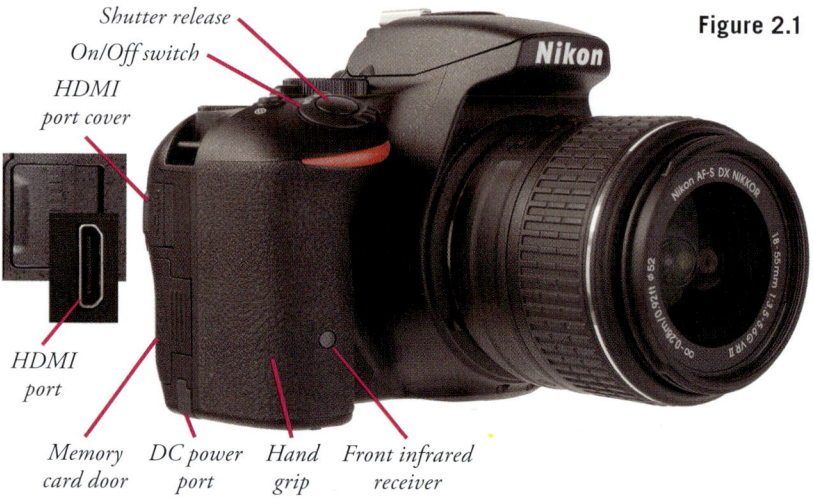

Shutter release
On/Off switch
HDMI port cover

Figure 2.1

HDMI port

Memory   DC power   Hand   Front infrared
card door   port   grip   receiver

- **Front infrared receiver.** This IR sensor receives a signal from the optional Nikon ML-L3 infrared remote control while standing in front of the camera (say, when you want to get in the picture yourself). A second IR sensor is on the back panel of the camera.

- **Hand grip.** This provides a comfortable hand hold, and also contains the D5500's battery.

- **HDMI port.** This small door can be opened to plug in an HDMI cable to connect your D5500 to an HDTV or other device. You need to buy an accessory cable to connect your D5500 to an HDTV, as one to fit this port is not provided with the camera.

- **Memory card door.** Your memory card can be inserted here when you slide the door toward the rear of the camera to open it.

- **DC power port.** Connect the optional AC adapter to the battery compartment through this opening.

Figure 2.2 shows a front view of the Nikon D5500 from the other side, with the electronic flash elevated. The controls here include:

- **Lens release button.** Press this button to unlock the lens, then rotate the lens away from the shutter release button to dismount your optics.

- **Lens mount index mark.** Line up the mark on the lens with this raised bump to align the lens when mounting it on the camera.

- **Lens autofocus/manual focus switch.** You can change from autofocus to manual using this switch.

Figure 2.2

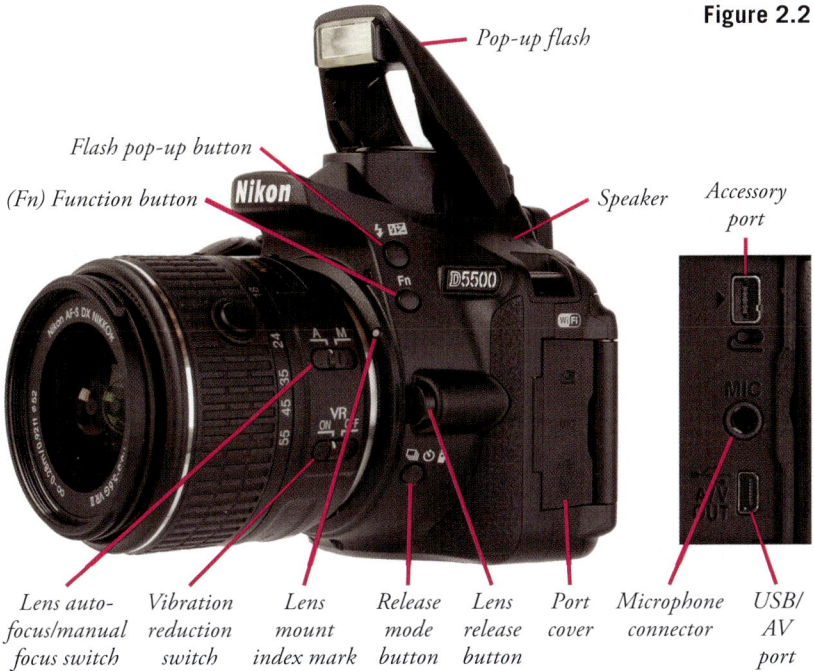

Pop-up flash

Flash pop-up button

(Fn) Function button

Speaker

Accessory port

Lens auto-focus/manual focus switch

Vibration reduction switch

Lens mount index mark

Release mode button

Lens release button

Port cover

Microphone connector

USB/AV port

- **Vibration reduction switch.** Turn your lens's image stabilization feature (if present) on or off using this switch.
- **Speaker.** Sounds emitted by the camera, including audio during movie clip playback, are produced here.
- **Port cover.** The rubber cover protects the USB/AV and microphone ports, and GPS/accessory terminals when not in use. (The HDMI port is under a similar cover on the opposite side of the camera.)
- **Fn (Function) button.** This conveniently located button activates ISO sensitivity settings, but can be programmed to perform any one of several other different actions instead, including adjustment of image quality, bracketing, or white balance.
- **Release mode button.** This conveniently located button allows you to switch among release modes. Press and rotate the command dial to switch among Single Frame, Continuous L, Continuous H, Self-Timer, 2s Delayed Remote, Quick Response Remote, and Quiet Shutter modes, described in more detail in Chapter 3.

Controls for using the D5500's built-in electronic flash (also called a strobe or Speedlight) are also shown in Figure 2.2. These components include:

■ **Pop-up flash.** The flash elevates from the top of the camera, theoretically reducing the chances of red-eye reflections, because the higher light source is less likely to reflect back from your subjects' eyes into the camera lens. In practice, the red-eye effect is still possible (and likely), and can be further minimized with the D5500's red-eye reduction lamp (which flashes before the exposure, causing the subjects' pupils to contract), and the after-shot red-eye elimination offered in the Retouch menu. (Your image editor may also have anti-red-eye tools.) Of course, the best strategy is to use an external Speedlight that mounts on the accessory shoe on top of the camera (and thus is even higher) or a flash that is off-camera entirely.

■ **Flash pop-up/Flash mode/Flash compensation button.** This button releases the built-in flash so it can flip up and start the charging process. If you decide you do not want to use the flash, you can turn it off by pressing the flash head back down. This button is held down while spinning the command dial to choose flash mode. You'll find more on flash compensation in Chapter 5.

The main feature on the side of the Nikon D5500 is a rubber cover that protects the three connector ports underneath from dust and moisture. In the figure you can also see the neck strap connector, and switches on the lens to adjust for autofocus/manual focus and to turn vibration reduction (VR) on or off. The connector ports, shown in Figure 2.2, with the cover removed, are as follows:

■ **USB/AV port.** Plug in the USB cable furnished with your Nikon D5500 and connect the other end to a USB port in your computer to transfer photos, to upload Picture Control settings, or to upload/download other settings between your camera and computer. The included AV cable can be connected to link the camera to a standard-definition television or monitor to view your photos and movies on a large screen. Connect the red/white RCA plugs on the cable to the audio input jacks of your monitor/TV, and the yellow plug to the video jack.

■ **Accessory port.** Connect the optional Nikon GP-1a Global Positioning Service device here, or plug in the MC-DC2 wired remote control here or WR-10 wireless remote, instead. If you want to use both, connect the GP-1a and then plug the remote into a pass-through connector on the GPS device.

■ **Microphone connector.** Although the D5500 has built-in stereo micro-phones on the top panel, if you want better quality (and want to shield your video clip soundtracks from noises emanating from the camera and/or your handling of it), you can plug in an accessory mic here.

The Nikon D5500's Back Panel

The back panel of the Nikon D5500 bristles with almost a dozen different controls, buttons, and knobs. That might seem like a lot of controls to learn, but you'll find that it's a lot easier to press a dedicated button and spin a dial than to jump to a menu every time you want to access one of these features. You can see the controls clustered along the top edge of the back panel in Figure 2.3 and those on the right side in Figure 2.4. The key buttons and components and their functions are as follows:

■ **Rear infrared receiver.** This second IR sensor receives a signal from the optional Nikon ML-L3 infrared remote control while standing behind the camera. The other IR receiver is located on the front of the camera. You can specify the period of time the D5500 "looks" for IR signals when you switch to remote control release mode (as described in Chapter 1). Select from 1, 5, 10, or 15 minutes using Custom Setting c4, as I'll explain in Chapter 4.

■ **MENU/Reset #1 button.** Summons/exits the menu displayed on the rear LCD of the D5500. When you're working with submenus, this button also serves to exit a submenu and return to the main menu. Holding down this button at the same time as the Info/Reset #2 button returns the set-tings of your camera to their default values.

Figure 2.3

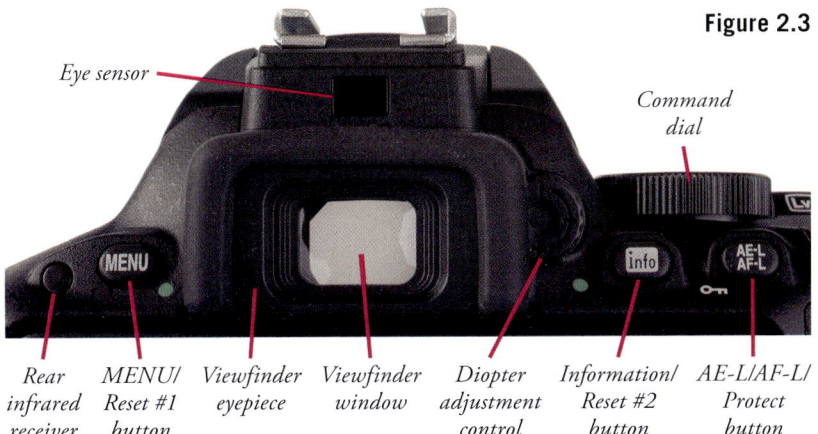

Eye sensor

Command dial

MENU

info

AE-L
AF-L

| Rear infrared receiver | MENU/ Reset #1 button | Viewfinder eyepiece | Viewfinder window | Diopter adjustment control | Information/ Reset #2 button | AE-L/AF-L/ Protect button |

- **Information/Reset #2 button.** Turns the LCD display on/off and, when used with the MENU button, can be used to reset the camera. Don't confuse it with the *i* (Information Edit) button on the back panel of the camera to the right of the LCD monitor, described shortly. Note that Nikon doesn't assign "Reset #1" or "Reset #2" nomenclature to these buttons; I've done so to help differentiate between the two.

- **Eye sensor.** Turns off the LCD when you bring the camera up to your eye (or when anything else approaches the sensor; a potential annoyance). The eye sensor can save some power, and is handy in some situations, such as when those around you might find the illuminated monitor annoying.

- **Viewfinder eyepiece/window.** You can frame your composition by peering into the viewfinder. It's surrounded by a soft rubber frame that seals out extraneous light when pressing your eye tightly up to the viewfinder, and it also protects your eyeglass lenses (if worn) from scratching. It can be removed and replaced by the DK-5 eyepiece cap when you use the camera on a tripod, to ensure that light coming from the back of the camera doesn't venture inside and possibly affect the exposure reading. Shielding the viewfinder with your hand may be more convenient (unless you're using the self-timer to get in the photo yourself).

- **Diopter adjustment control.** Rotate this to adjust the diopter correction for your eyesight.

- **AE-L/AF-L (autoexposure/autofocus lock)/Protect button.** This button can be programmed by you to provide a variety of autoexposure/autofocus locking functions, which I'll explain in Chapter 4. By default, it locks the exposure or focus that the camera sets when you partially depress the shutter button. The exposure lock indication (AE-L icon) appears in the viewfinder. If you want to recalculate exposure or autofocus with the shutter button still partially depressed, press the button again. The exposure/autofocus will be unlocked when you release the shutter button or take the picture. To retain the exposure/autofocus lock for subsequent photos, keep the button pressed while shooting. This double-duty button also can be used to protect an image from accidental erasure when reviewing a picture on the LCD. Press once to protect the image, a second time to unprotect it. A key symbol appears when the image is displayed to show that it is protected. (This feature safeguards an image from erasure when deleting or transferring pictures only; when you format a card, protected images are removed along with all the others.)

■ **Command dial.** This is the main control dial of the D5500, used to set or adjust most functions, such as shutter speed, bracketing sequence, white balance, ISO, and so forth, either alone or when another button is depressed simultaneously. It is often used in conjunction with the exposure compensation/aperture button on top of the camera when pairs of settings can be made, such as exposure (command dial: shutter speed; exposure compensation/aperture button+command dial: aperture).

You'll be using the buttons to the right of the LCD monitor quite frequently, so learn their functions now.

■ **Playback button.** Press to summon the most recently shot image to the LCD monitor. Press again to return to shooting mode (or just tap the shutter release).

■ **Information edit (*i*) button.** Press this button to activate the information edit display. To change any of the parameters in the bottom rows of the display, use the multi selector directional buttons to highlight the option. Then, press OK to summon a screen that lets you make the changes. Or, press again to remove the information display (or simply tap the shutter release button). The display will also clear after the period you've set for LCD display (the default value is 20 seconds). I'll describe the use of the shooting information display in more detail later in this chapter. Don't confuse this button with the Info button next to the viewfinder, which simply turns the LCD display on or off.

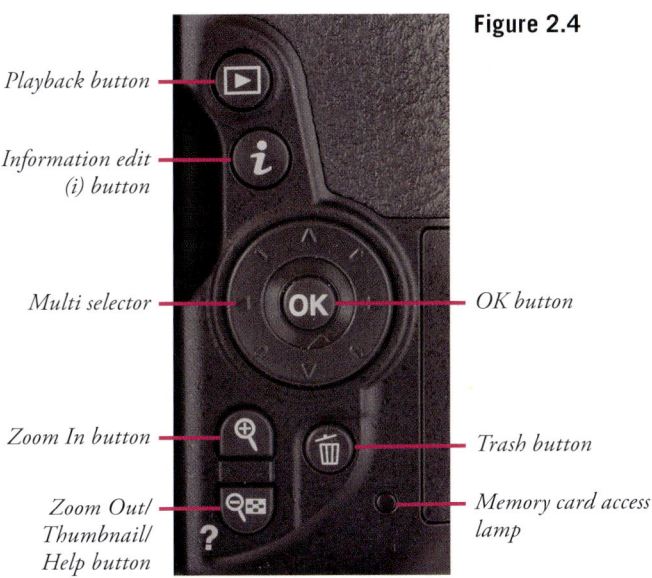

Figure 2.4

Playback button

Information edit (i) button

Multi selector

OK button

Zoom In button

Trash button

Zoom Out/ Thumbnail/ Help button

Memory card access lamp

- **Multi selector.** This joypad-like button can be moved up, down, side to side, or pressed. It can be used for several functions, including AF-point selection, scrolling around a magnified image, trimming a photo, or setting white balance correction. Within menus, pressing the up/down arrows moves the on-screen cursor up or down; pressing toward the right selects the highlighted item and displays its options; pressing left cancels and returns to the previous menu. During image review, the up/down buttons change the type of information displayed about each image.

- **OK button.** Press to confirm your selections, and to display the current review image in the Date list and Thumbnail list displays.

- **Memory card access lamp.** When lit or blinking, this lamp indicates that a memory card is being accessed.

- **Zoom Out/Thumbnail/Help button.** During image review, use this button to change from full-screen view to 4, 12, or 80 thumbnails, calendar view, or to zoom out. I'll explain zooming and other playback options in the next section. When viewing most menu items on the LCD, pressing this button produces a concise Help screen with tips on how to make the relevant setting. Note that if you have the touch screen activated, you can also use a stretching motion with two fingers on the screen to zoom out.

- **Zoom In button.** Press to zoom in on an image, and to select image quality settings. A pinching motion on the LCD monitor can also be used to zoom in.

- **Trash button.** Press to erase the image shown on the LCD. A display will pop up on the LCD asking you to press the Trash button once more to delete the photo, or press the Playback button to cancel.

Playing Back Images

Here are the basics involved in reviewing images on the LCD monitor screen (or on a television screen you have connected with a cable).

- **Start review.** To begin review, press the Playback button at the right of the LCD. The most recently viewed image will appear on the LCD.

- **Playback folder.** Image review generally shows you the images in the currently selected folder on your Secure Digital card. A given card can contain several folders (a new one is created anytime you exceed 999 images in the current folder). You can use the Playback folder menu option in the Playback menu (as I'll explain in Chapter 3) to select a specific folder or direct the D5500 to display images from all the folders on the memory card.

■ **View thumbnail images.** To change the view from a single image to four, 12, or 80 thumbnails, press the Zoom Out button. Full instructions are displayed in the "Viewing Thumbnails" section that follows.

■ **Zoom in and out.** To zoom in or out, press the Zoom In or Zoom Out/ Thumbnail button, following the instructions in the "Zooming the Nikon D5500 Playback Display" in the next section. (It also shows you how to move the zoomed area around using the multi selector keypad.)

■ **Move back and forth.** To advance to the next image, press the right edge of the multi selector pad or rotate the command dial to the right; to go back to a previous shot, press the left edge or rotate the command dial left. When you reach the beginning/end of the photos in your folder, the display "wraps around" to the end/beginning of the available shots.

■ **See different types of data.** To change the type of information about the displayed image that is shown, press the up and down portions of the multi selector pad.

■ **Remove images.** To delete an image that's currently on the screen, press the Trash button once, then press it again to confirm the deletion. To select and delete a group of images, use the Delete option in the Playback menu to specify particular photos to remove, as described in more detail in Chapter 3.

■ **Cancel playback.** To cancel image review, press the Playback button again, or simply tap the shutter release button.

Zooming the Nikon D5500 Playback Display

Here's how to zoom in on and out of your images during picture review:

1. When an image is displayed (use the Playback button to start), press the Zoom In button to fill the screen with a slightly magnified version of the image. (Or, with the touch screen, use a spreading motion with two fingers.)

2. A navigation window appears in the lower-right corner of the LCD showing the entire image. Keep pressing to continue zooming in to the maximum of 33X enlargement, with a full-resolution large image. (Medium and Small images zoom in to 25X and 13X, respectively.)

3. A yellow box in the navigation window shows the zoomed area within the full image. The entire navigation window vanishes from the screen after a few seconds, leaving you with a full-screen view of the zoomed portion of the image. (See Figure 2.5.)

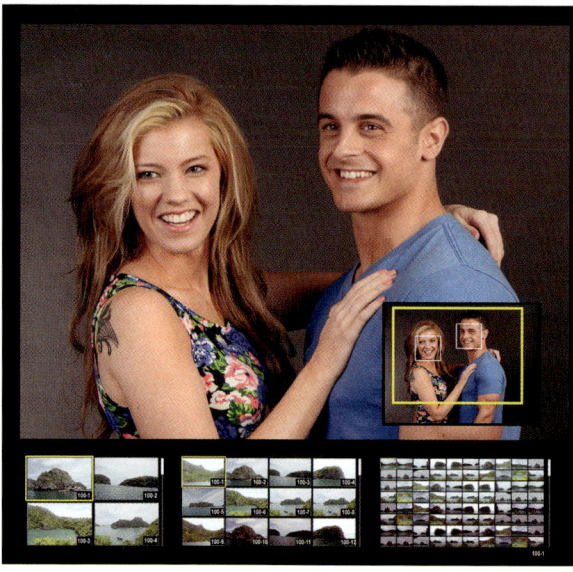

Figure 2.5

4. To detect faces, use the multi selector buttons while an image is zoomed to highlight the main face in the image. See the sidebar that follows, "Playback Face Detection" to learn about your options.

5. Use the command dial to move to the same zoomed area of the next/ previous image.

6. Use the Zoom Out/Thumbnail button to zoom back out of the image, or use a pinching motion with two fingers on the touch screen.

7. Use the multi selector buttons or a swiping motion on the touch screen to move the zoomed area around within the image. The navigation window will reappear for reference when zooming or scrolling around within the display.

8. To the exit zoom in/zoom out display, keep pressing the Zoom Out button until the full screen/full image/information display appears again, or use the pinching motion on the touch screen, or simply tap the image with a single finger.

PLAYBACK FACE DETECTION

When zooming in on an image during playback, the D5500 detects human faces that are looking toward the camera, indicated by white boxes within the small navigation window in the lower-right corner. You can then access the following options by first pressing the information edit (*i*) button:

■ While zoomed, after pressing the *i* button, you can press the OK button to zoom in further on the "main" face in the image. If only one face appears, it will have the white box around it. If more than one face is surrounded by a white box, the screen doesn't visually differentiate between the "main" and "secondary" faces, but when you press the OK button, you'll find out, as the image zooms in even more. To return to the previous zoom view, press the *i* button again.

■ While zoomed, you can press the *i* button alone to toggle Face Detection on or off. An indicator at the bottom left of the screen shows whether the feature is active or not.

■ As you view a zoomed image, you can press the *i* button and then use the multi selector to switch to other faces. Although there is no indication as to which is the new "main" face in the navigation thumbnail, the zoomed view will shift to move the selected face closer to the center of the LCD monitor.

Viewing Thumbnails

The Nikon D5500 provides other options for reviewing images in addition to zooming in and out. Pages of thumbnail images offer a way to scroll through a large number of pictures quickly to find the one you want to examine in more detail. The D5500 lets you switch quickly from single- to four- to 12- to 80-image views, with a scroll bar displayed at the right side of the screen to show you the relative position of the displayed thumbnails within the full collection of images in the active folder on your memory card. Figure 2.5 (bottom) offers a comparison between the three levels of thumbnail views: four thumbnails (bottom left), twelve thumbnails (bottom center), or 80 thumbnails (bottom right). The Zoom In and Zoom Out buttons or touch screen controls are used.

■ **Add thumbnails.** To increase the number of thumbnails on the screen, press the Zoom Out button. The D5500 will switch from single image to four thumbnails to 12 thumbnails to 80 thumbnails, and then on to calendar view, described next. (The display doesn't cycle back to single image again.)

- **Reduce number of thumbnails.** To decrease the number of thumbnails on the screen, press the Zoom In button to change from calendar view to 80 thumbnails to 12 thumbnails to four thumbnails, or from four thumbnails to single-image display. Continuing to press the Zoom In button once you've returned to single-image display starts the zoom process described in the previous section.

- **Switch between thumbnails and full image.** When viewing thumbnails, you can quickly switch between thumbnail view and full-image display by pressing the OK button in the center of the multi selector. Pressing it again brings up the Retouch menu (described in Chapter 4). If you want to return to thumbnail views instead, press the Zoom In button.

- **Change highlighted thumbnail area.** Use the multi selector to move the yellow highlight box around among the thumbnails.

- **Protect and delete images.** When viewing thumbnails or a single page image, press the Protect button to preserve the image against accidental deletion (a small key icon is overlaid on the top-left corner of the full-page image; press Protect again to remove protection).

- **Exit image review.** Tap the shutter release button or press the Playback button to exit image review. You don't have to worry about missing a shot because you were reviewing images; a half-press of the shutter release automatically returns the D5500 to picture-taking mode.

Working with Calendar View

When you're in 80 thumbnail mode, pressing the Zoom Out button one more time takes you to calendar view, where you can sort through images arranged by the date they were taken. This feature is especially useful when you're traveling and want to see only the pictures you took in, say, a particular city on a certain day.

- **View dates and images taken on that date.** A yellow highlight box appears around a selected date in the date list calendar, as shown in Figure 2.6. When there are images available that were taken on that date, a scrolling thumbnail column appears at the right of the screen. The thumbnail column disappears if there are no photos taken on the highlighted date.

- **Change dates.** Use the multi selector keys to move through the date list.

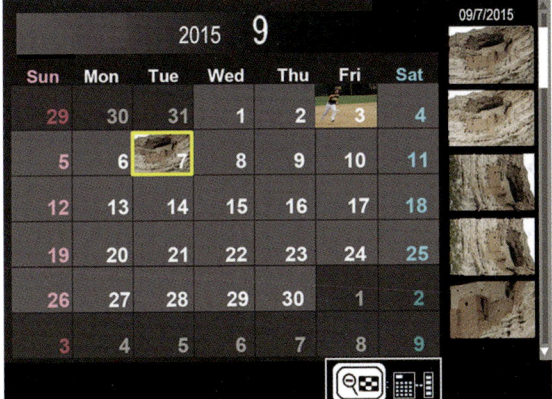

Figure 2.6
Calendar view allows you to browse through all images on your memory card taken on a certain date.

- **View a date's images.** Press the Zoom In button to toggle between the date list to the scrolling thumbnail list of images taken on that date at the right of the screen. When viewing the thumbnail list, you can use the multi selector up/down keys to scroll through the available images. Press the Zoom In button again to return to the date list calendar when you want to select a different date.

- **Preview an image.** In the thumbnail list, when you've highlighted an image you want to look at, press the Zoom In button to see an enlarged view of that image without leaving the calendar view mode. The zoomed image replaces the date list.

- **Delete images.** Pressing the Trash button deletes a highlighted image in the thumbnail list. In the date view, pressing the Trash button removes all the images taken on that date (use with caution!).

- **Exit calendar view.** In thumbnail list view, if you highlight an image and press the OK button, you'll exit calendar view and the highlighted image will be shown on the LCD in the display mode you've chosen. In date list view, pressing the Zoom In button exits calendar view and returns to 80 thumbnails view. You can also exit calendar view by tapping the shutter release or by pressing the MENU or Playback buttons.

Working with the Shooting Information/ Photo Data Displays

Your Nikon D5500 can display two types of information on the color LCD monitor as you are reviewing or taking pictures:

- **Shooting information display.** This is the screen of information that provides a readout of various settings for the D5500's shooting parameters. (See Figure 1.7, left, in the previous chapter.) It appears when you press the *i* button on the back of the camera, just to the right of the LCD monitor.

- **Photo Data.** These are a series of up to eight screens (including GPS data, which appears only if you used a GPS device to take the picture) that provide various types of shooting and other information *about a particular image* that you are reviewing. The data shown applies only to that image, and does not reflect your D5500's current shooting settings (unless you're viewing an image you've just taken).

Using the Shooting Information Display

The shooting information display appears when you press the Info button to the right of the color LCD monitor. Hide this display by pressing the Info button, or by tapping the shutter release button. The shooting information display provides a lot of basic shooting data. By pressing the information edit button located on the back of the camera when the shooting information screen is displayed, you can change many settings, including:

- **Image quality.** Choose JPEG Fine, Normal, Basic, RAW, or RAW+JPEG Fine, Normal, or Basic.
- **Image size.** Select from Large, Medium, or Small resolutions.
- **White balance.** Choose any of the white balance modes, including Auto and Preset, as described in Chapter 3.
- **ISO sensitivity.** Select ISO sensitivity from ISO 100 to ISO 25600.
- **Release mode.** Choose one of the release modes described in Chapter 1, including single frame, continuous, self-timer, delayed remote, quick-response remote, and quiet shutter release.
- **Autofocus mode.** Select from AF-S, AF-C, and AF-A autofocus modes.
- **AF-area mode.** Choose single-point AF-area mode, dynamic-area AF (9 points), dynamic-area AF (21 points), dynamic-area AF (39 points), 3D-tracking, and Auto-area AF.
- **Metering mode.** Select from Matrix, Center-weighted, and Spot metering.

- **Active D-Lighting.** Choose to extend the dynamic range of your image to one of four levels (Low, Normal, High, Extra High), plus Off.

- **Bracketing increment.** Select a bracketing increment for 0.3 (one-third stop) to 2 full stops, or off.

- **Flash mode.** You can choose a flash mode, including flash on, red-eye, slow sync with red-eye prevention, slow sync, and rear sync. When the flash is elevated, you can also choose one of these modes by pressing the flash button and rotating the command dial. The selected mode will be displayed on the shooting information screen.

- **Flash exposure compensation.** You can choose a flash exposure compensation amount from –3 to +1 EV. When the flash is elevated, you can also choose flash compensation by holding down the flash button and the aperture/compensation button and rotating the command dial. The selected mode will be displayed on the shooting information screen.

- **Exposure compensation.** You can choose an exposure compensation amount from –5 to +5 EV. You can also choose exposure compensation by holding down the aperture/compensation button and rotating the command dial. The selected mode will be displayed on the shooting information screen.

- **Picture Control.** Choose a Picture Control style.

Using the Photo Data Displays

When reviewing an image on the screen, your D5500 can supplement the image itself with a variety of shooting data, ranging from basic information presented at the bottom of the LCD monitor display to text overlays that detail virtually every shooting option you've selected.

You can change the *types* of information displayed using the Display Mode entry in the Playback menu. There you will find check boxes you can mark for both basic photo information (overexposed highlights and the focus point used when the image was captured) and detailed photo information (which includes an RGB histogram and various data screens). To change to any of these views while an image is on the screen in Playback mode, press the multi selector up/down buttons.

- **Image only.** If you specify None in the Playback menu's Display Mode entry, the D5500 will add a screen that shows only the image itself, with no extraneous information. (It does not nullify the other screens, in other words. You get an additional plain-vanilla screen.) I'm not providing a figure that illustrates this mode.

- **File information screen.** The basic full-image review display is officially called the file information screen, and looks like Figure 2.7. Press the multi selector down button to advance to the next information screen.

- **Overview data.** This screen, shown in Figure 2.8, provides a smaller image of your photo, but more information, including a luminance (brightness) histogram, metering mode used, lens focal length, exposure compensation, flash compensation, and lots of other data that's self-explanatory.

- **Highlights.** When highlights display is active (after being chosen in the Display Mode entry of the Playback menu, described in Chapter 3), any overexposed areas will be indicated by a flashing black border. As I am unable to make the printed page flash, you'll have to check out this effect for yourself. You can visualize what these "blinkies" look like in Figure 2.9, left.

- **RGB histogram.** Another optional screen is the RGB histogram, which you can see in Figure 2.9, right.

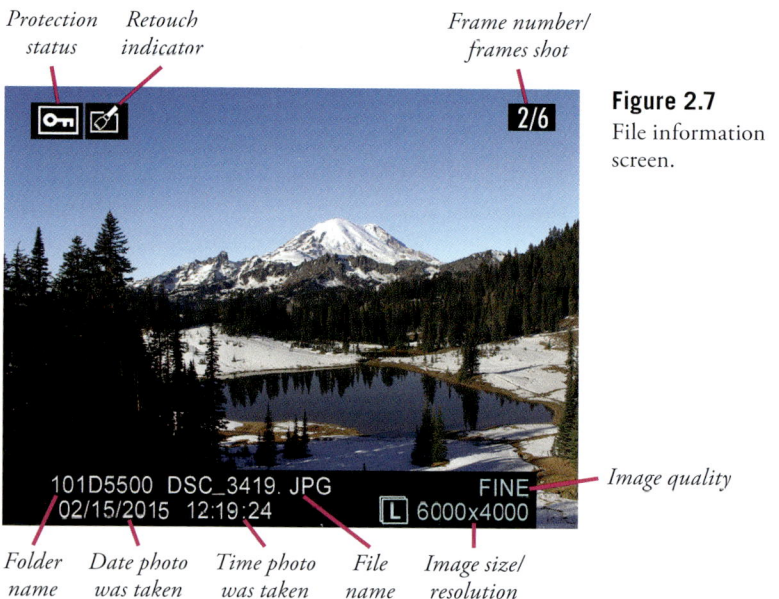

Protection status   Retouch indicator   Frame number/ frames shot

Figure 2.7
File information screen.

Image quality

Folder name   Date photo was taken   Time photo was taken   File name   Image size/ resolution

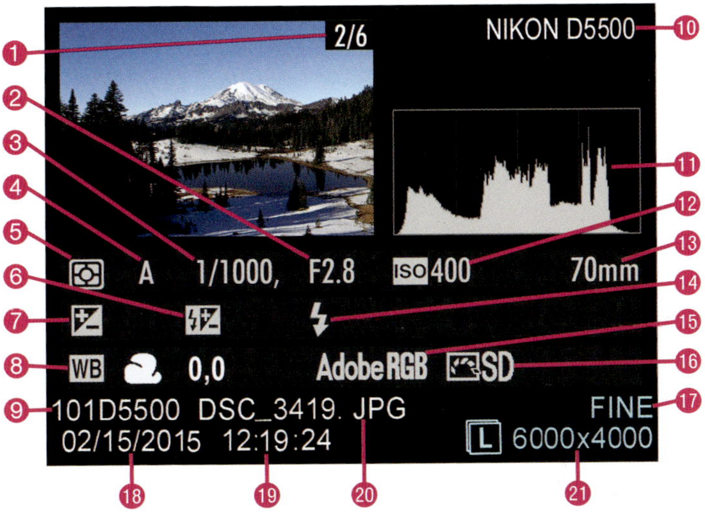

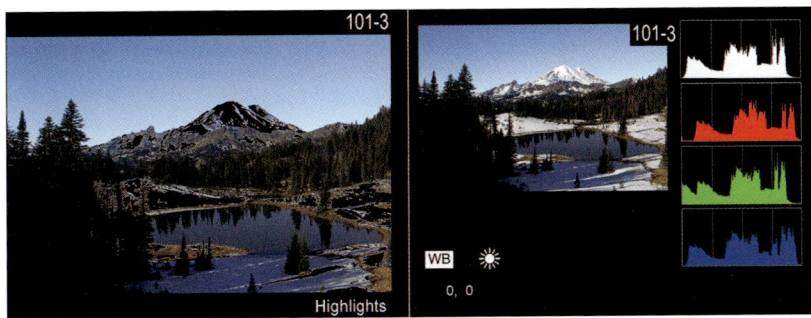

2/6   NIKON D5500

A 1/1000, F2.8 ISO 400 70mm

WB 0,0 Adobe RGB SD

101D5500 DSC_3419.JPG FINE
02/15/2015 12:19:24 L 6000x4000

① Frame number/frames shot
② Aperture
③ Shutter speed
④ Exposure mode
⑤ Metering method
⑥ Flash compensation
⑦ Exposure compensation

⑧ White balance adjustments
⑨ Folder name
⑩ Camera name
⑪ Luminance (brightness) histogram
⑫ ISO setting
⑬ Lens focal length
⑭ Flash mode

⑮ Color space
⑯ Picture control
⑰ JPEG image quality
⑱ Date photo taken
⑲ Time photo taken
⑳ File name
㉑ Size (resolution)

Figure 2.8 Overview data screen.

101-3   101-3

WB   ☼
0, 0

Highlights

Figure 2.9 Highlights screen (left); RGB histogram (right).

- **Shooting Data 1.** This is the first in a series of three screens that collectively provide everything else you might want to know about a picture you've taken. I'm not providing any labels in Figure 2.10, because the information in the first seven lines in the screen should be obvious.

- **Shooting Data 2.** This screen shows white balance data and adjustments, the color space you've selected, and lists any Picture Control tweaks you've entered. (See Figure 2.10, right.)

- **Shooting Data 3.** The next screen shows any noise reduction you've specified, Active D-Lighting status, and any Retouch menu changes you may have made. Although none of them apply to the background image shown in Figure 2.11, left. I've added a few entries to show the kind of changes that can be made.

- **GPS data.** This screen appears *only* if the image was taken using the GPS. It includes latitude, longitude, altitude, and time information, as shown in Figure 2.11, right.

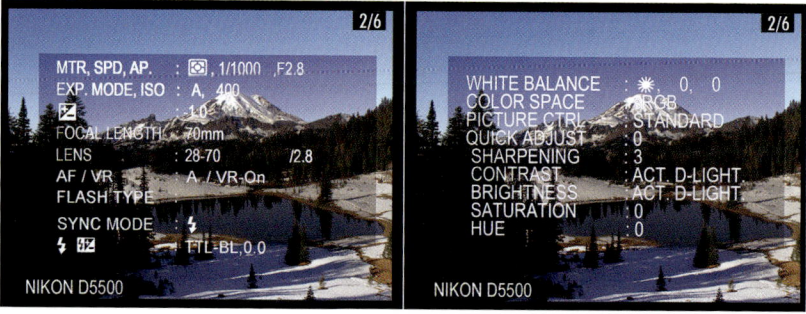

Figure 2.10 Shooting Data 1 (left); Shooting Data 2 (right).

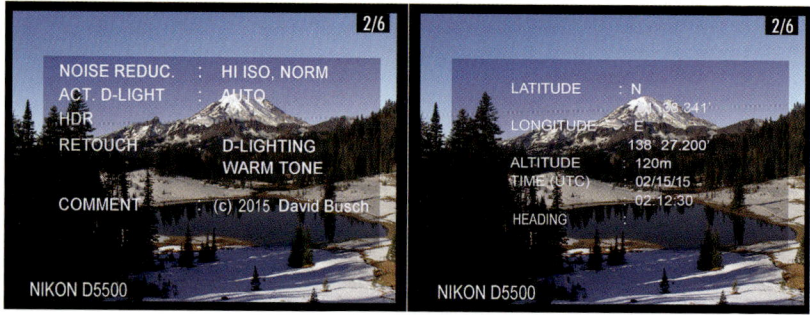

Figure 2.11 Shooting Data 3 (left); GPS data (right).

Going Topside

The top surface of the Nikon D5500 (see Figure 2.12) has its own set of frequently accessed controls.

- **Sensor focal plane indicator.** This indicator on the left side of the top panel shows the *plane* of the sensor, for use in applications where exact measurement of the distance from the focal plane to the subject is necessary. (These are mostly scientific/close-up applications.)

- **Accessory shoe.** Slide an electronic flash into this mount when you need a more powerful Speedlight. A dedicated flash unit, like the Nikon SB-910, can use the multiple contact points shown to communicate exposure, zoom setting, white balance information, and other data between the flash and the camera. There's more on using electronic flash in Chapter 5. You can also mount other accessories on this shoe, such as the Nikon GP-1 GPS adapter.

- **Microphones.** The D5500 has a pair of stereo microphones built into the electronic flash housing on top of the camera, seen as a set of holes labeled L and R.

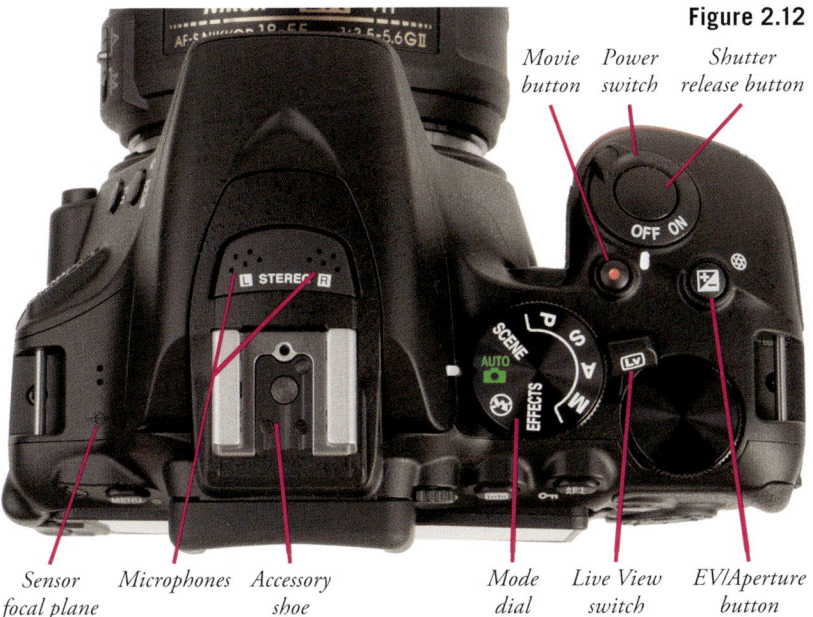

Figure 2.12

Movie   Power   Shutter
button   switch   release button

Sensor   Microphones   Accessory   Mode   Live View   EV/Aperture
focal plane   shoe   dial   switch   button
indicator

- **Mode dial.** Rotate this dial to select from two fully automatic modes (Auto and Auto (No Flash)), four advanced exposure modes (Manual, Aperture-priority, Shutter-priority, and Program), and additional modes (described in Chapter 1) selected by rotating the command dial to the SCENE or EFFECTS positions.

- **Power switch.** Rotate this switch clockwise to turn on the Nikon D5500 (and virtually all other Nikon dSLRs).

- **Shutter release button.** Partially depress this button to activate the exposure meter, lock in exposure, and focus (unless you've redefined the focus activation button, as outlined in Chapter 4). Press all the way to take the picture. Tapping the shutter release when the camera has turned off the autoexposure and autofocus mechanisms reactivates both. When a review image is displayed on the back-panel color LCD, tapping this button removes the image from the display and reactivates the autoexposure and autofocus mechanisms.

- **Exposure compensation/aperture button.** Hold down this button and spin the command dial to add or subtract exposure when using Program, Aperture-priority, or Shutter-priority modes. (In Manual mode, the exposure remains the same, but the "ideal" exposure shown in the electronic analog display [more on that in the next section] is modified to reflect the extra/reduced exposure you're calling for.) The button is also used to make secondary settings, such as aperture when the camera is in Manual exposure mode. (The command dial changes shutter speed, and holding down the aperture button while rotating the command dial changes aperture.)

- **Live View switch.** Rotate this momentary-contact switch toward the back of the camera to turn on live view and enable movie shooting. Rotate it again to turn live view/moving shooting off.

- **Movie button.** Press the red button to start movie shooting, and again to stop shooting.

Lens Components

The lens shown at left in Figure 2.13 is a typical lens that might be mounted on a Nikon dSLR, the 18-140mm kit lens often sold with the D5500. Unfortunately, this particular lens doesn't include all the common features found on the various Nikon lenses available for your camera, so I am including a second lens (shown at right in the figure) that *does* have more features and components. It's not a typical lens that a D5500 user might work with, however. This 17-35mm zoom is a pricey "pro" lens that costs about twice as much as the entire D5500 camera. Nevertheless, it makes a good example.

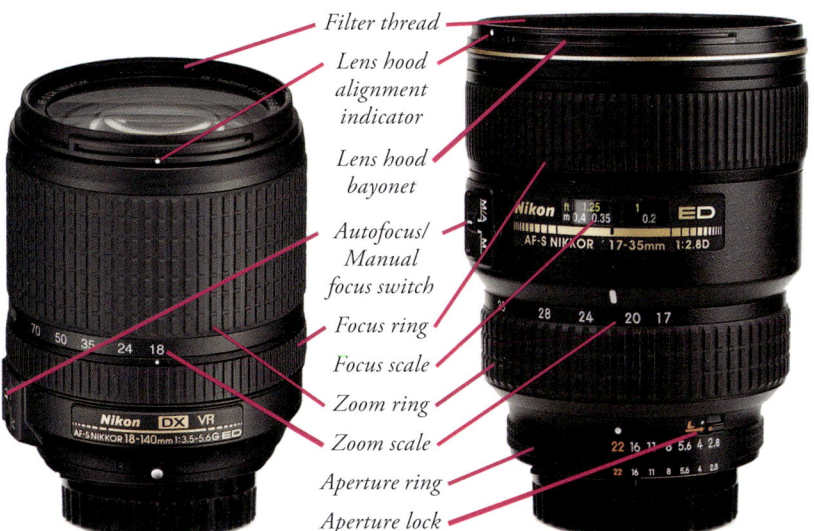

Filter thread
Lens hood
alignment
indicator
Lens hood
bayonet
Autofocus/
Manual
focus switch
Focus ring
Focus scale
Zoom ring
Zoom scale
Aperture ring
Aperture lock

Figure 2.13

Components found on this pair of lenses include:

■ **Filter thread.** Most lenses have a thread on the front for attaching filters and other add-ons. Some also use this thread for attaching a lens hood (you screw on the filter first, and then attach the hood to the screw thread on the front of the filter). Some lenses, such as the AF-S Nikkor 14-24mm f/2.8G ED lens, have no front filter thread, either because their front elements are too curved to allow mounting a filter and/or because the front element is so large that huge filters would be prohibitively expensive. Some of these front-filter-hostile lenses allow using smaller filters that drop into a slot at the back of the lens.

■ **Lens hood bayonet.** Lenses like the 17-35mm zoom shown in the figure use this bayonet to mount the lens hood. Such lenses generally will have a dot on the edge showing how to align the lens hood with the bayonet mount.

■ **Focus ring.** This is the ring you turn when you manually focus the lens, or fine-tune autofocus adjustment. It's a narrow ring at the very front of the lens (on the 18-55mm kit lens, for example), or a wider ring located somewhere else.

- **Focus scale.** This is a readout found on many lenses that rotates in unison with the lens's focus mechanism to show the distance at which the lens has been focused. It's a useful indicator for double-checking autofocus, roughly evaluating depth-of-field, and for setting manual focus guesstimates.

- **Zoom scale.** These markings on the lens show the current focal length selected.

- **Zoom ring.** Turn this ring to change the zoom setting.

- **Autofocus/Manual focus switch.** Allows you to change from automatic focus to manual focus.

- **Aperture ring.** Some lenses have a ring that allows you to set a specific f/stop manually, rather than use the camera's internal electronic aperture control. An aperture ring is useful when a lens is mounted on a non-automatic extension ring, bellows, or other accessory that doesn't couple electronically with the camera. Aperture rings also allow using a lens on an older camera that lacks electronic control. In recent years, Nikon has been replacing lenses that have aperture rings with versions that only allow setting the aperture with camera controls.

- **Aperture lock.** If you want your D5500 (or other Nikon dSLR) to control the aperture electronically on a lens with an aperture ring, you must set the lens to its smallest aperture (usually f/22 or f/32) and lock it with this control.

- **Focus limit switch (not shown).** Some lenses have this switch, which limits the focus range of the lens, thus potentially reducing focus seeking when shooting distant subjects. The limiter stops the lens from trying to focus at closer distances (in this case, closer than 2.5 meters).

- **Vibration reduction switch (not shown).** Lenses with Nikon's Vibration Reduction (VR) feature include a switch for turning the stabilization feature on and off, and, in some cases, for changing from normal vibration reduction to a more aggressive "active" VR mode useful for, say, shooting from moving vehicles.

The back end of a lens intended for use on a Nikon camera has other components that you seldom see except when you swap lenses (and not illustrated here), but you still should know about:

- **Lens bayonet mount.** This is the mounting mechanism that attaches to a matching mount on the camera. Although the lens bayonet is usually metal, some lenses use a rugged plastic for this key component.

- **Automatic diaphragm lever.** This lever is moved by a matching lever in the camera to adjust the f/stop from wide open (which makes for the brightest view) to the *taking aperture* or *working aperture*, which is the f/stop that will be used to take the picture. The actual taking aperture is determined by the camera's metering system (or by you when the D5500 is in Manual mode), and is communicated to the lens through the electronic contacts described next. (An exception is when the aperture ring on the lens itself is unlocked and used to specify the f/stop.) However, the spring-loaded physical levers are what actually push the aperture to the selected f/stop.
- **Electronic contacts.** These metal contacts pass information to matching contacts in the camera body, allowing a firm electrical connection so that exposure, distance, and other information can be exchanged between the camera and lens.

Looking Inside the Viewfinder

Much of the important shooting status information is shown inside the viewfinder of the Nikon D5500. Not all of this information will be shown at any one time. Figure 2.14 shows what you can expect to see. These readouts include:

- **Focus points.** Can display the 39 areas used by the D5500 to focus. The camera can select the appropriate focus zone for you, or you can manually select one or all of the zones.
- **Active focus point.** The currently selected focus point can be highlighted with red illumination, depending on focus mode.
- **AF-area bracket.** Shows the area covered by the autofocus sensors.
- **Focus indicator.** This green dot appears when the subject covered by the active autofocus zone is in sharp focus, whether focus was achieved by the AF system, or by you using manual focusing. Left and right arrows show whether focus is set ahead of or behind the subject.
- **Autoexposure (AE) lock/Flash value lock indicator.** Shows that exposure or flash exposure has been locked.
- **Shutter speed.** Displays the current shutter speed selected by the camera, or by you in Manual exposure mode.
- **Aperture.** Shows the current aperture chosen by the D5500's autoexposure system, or specified by you when using Manual exposure mode.
- **Automatic ISO indicator.** Is shown as a reminder that the D5500 has been set to adjust ISO sensitivity automatically.

- **Flash compensation indicator.** Appears when flash EV changes have been made.
- **Exposure compensation indicator.** This is shown when exposure compensation (EV) changes have been made. It's easy to forget you've dialed in a little more or less exposure, and then shoot a whole series of pictures of a different scene that doesn't require such compensation. Beware!

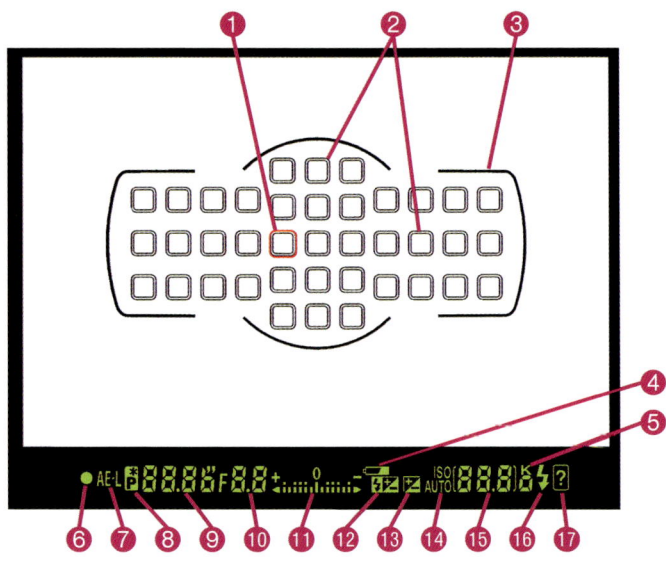

❶ Active focus point
❷ Focus points
❸ AF-area bracket
❹ Battery status
❺ Thousands of exposures
❻ Focus indicator
❼ Autoexposure/Flash value lock indicator
❽ Flexible program indicator

❾ Shutter speed
❿ Aperture
⓫ Exposure indicator/ Exposure compensation display/Electronic rangefinder
⓬ Flash compensation indicator
⓭ Exposure compensation indicator
⓮ Auto ISO indicator

⓯ Number of exposures remaining/Maximum burst available/ Number of shots remaining before buffer fills/White balance recording indicator/ Exposure compensation value/Flash compensation value/ISO sensitivity
⓰ Flash-ready indicator
⓱ Warning indicator

Figure 2.14

- **Electronic analog exposure display.** This scale shows the current exposure level, with the bottom indicator centered when the exposure is correct as metered. The indicator may also move to the left or right to indicate over- or underexposure (respectively). The scale is also used to show the amount of exposure compensation dialed in. It also shows exposure compensation and degree of horizontal tilt.

- **Exposures remaining/maximum burst available/other data.** This normally displays the number of exposures remaining on your memory card, but while shooting it changes to show a number that indicates the number of frames that can be taken in continuous shooting mode using the current settings. This indicator also shows other information, such as ISO sensitivity, exposure compensation value, and Active D-Lighting amount.

- **Thousands of exposures.** Displayed when more than 999 exposures remain; the readout to the left will then show number of shots remaining in thousands.

- **Flash-ready indicator.** This icon appears when the flash is fully charged.

- **Battery status.** Shows amount of remaining power.

- **Bracketing indicator.** Shows when Active D-Lighting, exposure, flash, or white balance bracketing is underway.

- **Warning indicator.** A flashing question mark indicator appears when any of several errors occurs, such as lens not attached, low battery level, no memory card/damaged or locked memory card, or camera's internal clock needs to be reset.

Underneath Your Nikon D5500

There's not a lot going on with the bottom panel of your Nikon D5500. You'll find the battery compartment access door and a tripod socket, which secures the camera to a tripod. The socket accepts other accessories, such as quick-release plates that allow rapid attaching and detaching of the D5500 from a matching platform affixed to your tripod.

Chapter 3

Playback and Shooting Menu Settings

The Playback and Shooting menus determine how the D5500 displays images on review, and how it uses many of its shooting features to take a photo. You'll find the Custom Setting, Setup, Retouch, and My Menu options in Chapter 4.

Anatomy of the Nikon D5500's Menus

Press the MENU button, located to the left of the viewfinder, to access the menu system. The most recently accessed menu will appear.

- **Access menus.** Press the MENU button to display the main menu screens.
- **Navigate menus.** Next, use your favorite navigation method to locate the setting you want to work with:
  - **Touch screen.** Tap the icons in the left column to select the top-level menu you want to use. Then tap a specific menu entry to jump to that item, and tap again to select any submenu entries. The Return icon (a reverse-pointing arrow) will appear in the upper-right corner of the submenu to allow you to back up to the previous screen.
  - **Button navigation.** Use the multi selector's left/right/up/down buttons to navigate among the menu entries to highlight your choice. Moving the highlighting to the left column lets you scroll up and down among the six top-level menus, as described next.
- **Learn the top-level menus.** From the top left in Figure 3.1, they are Playback, Shooting, Custom Setting, Setup, Retouch, and My Menu, with Help access represented by a question mark at the bottom of the column.

A selected top-level menu's icon will change from black-and-white to yellow highlighting. Use the multi selector's right button to move into the column containing that menu's choices, and the top-level icon will change once again, to the color associated with that menu (Playback: Blue; Shooting: Green; Custom Setting: Red; Setup: Orange; Retouch: Purple; My Menu: Gray). Use the up/down buttons to scroll among the entries. If more than one screen full of choices is available, a scroll bar appears at the far right of the screen, with a position slider showing the relative position of the currently highlighted entry.

- **Access entry.** To work with a highlighted menu entry, press the OK button in the center of the multi selector, or just press the right button on the multi selector. Any additional screens of choices will appear. You can move among them using the same multi selector movements.

- **Confirm selection.** You can confirm a selection by pressing the OK button or, frequently, by pressing the right button on the multi selector once again. Some functions require scrolling to a Done menu choice, or include an instruction to set a choice using some other button.

- **Back out.** Pressing the multi selector left button (or tapping the Return icon at upper right) usually backs you out of the current screen, and pressing the MENU button again usually does the same thing. You can exit the menu system at any time by tapping the shutter release button, too.

- **Deja view.** The Nikon D5500 "remembers" the top-level menu and specific menu entry you were using (but not any submenus) the last time the menu system was accessed, so pressing the MENU button brings you back to where you left off.

Playback Menu Options

The blue-coded Playback menu has ten entries related to the display, review, and printing of the photos you've taken. (Eight are shown in Figure 3.1.) The choices you'll find include:

- Delete
- Playback Folder
- Playback Display Options
- Image Review
- Auto Image Rotation
- Rotate Tall
- Slide Show
- DPOF Print Order
- Rating
- Select to Send to Smart Device

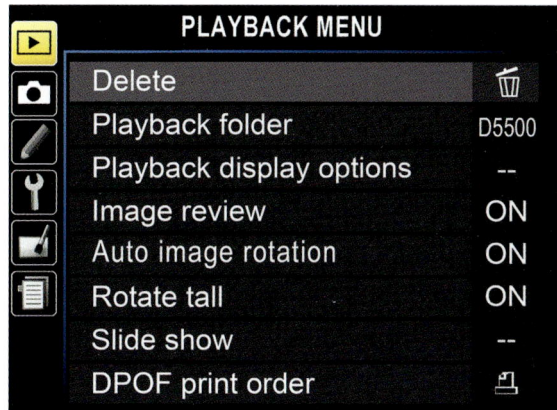

Figure 3.1
Playback menu.

Delete

Options: Selected, Select Date, and All

My preference: N/A

You're given three choices: Selected, Select Date, and All. To delete only some pictures from a folder, choose Selected; you'll see an image selection screen like the one shown in Figure 3.2. Then, follow these instructions:

1. **Scroll.** Use the multi selector cursor keys to scroll among the available images. You can also scroll by sliding a finger up or down the touch screen and tapping on an image to highlight it.

2. **Zoom in.** When you highlight an image you think you might like to delete, press the Zoom In button to temporarily enlarge that image so you can evaluate it further. When you release the Zoom In button, the selection screen returns. You can also zoom in by tapping the Zoom icon at the bottom of the screen; however, to zoom back out you must either tap the Return icon in the upper-right corner, or press the OK button. I find it's much easier to simply press and release the Zoom In button rather than resort to the touch screen.

3. **Mark images.** To mark an image for deletion, press the Zoom Out button (*not* the Trash button). A trash can icon will appear overlaid on that image's thumbnail. To unmark an image, press the Zoom Out button again. You can also tap the highlighted thumbnail to mark it for deletion, and unmark it with another tap.

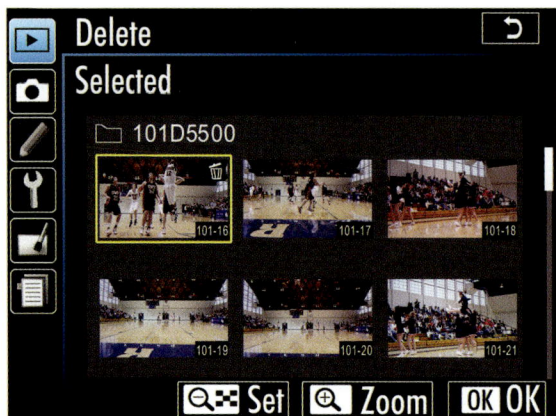

Figure 3.2
Images selected for deletion are marked with a trash can icon.

4. **Confirm.** When you've finished marking images to delete, press OK or tap the OK icon at the bottom of the screen. A final screen will appear asking you to confirm the removal of the image(s). Choose Yes to delete the image(s) or No to cancel deletion, and then press OK. If you selected Yes, then you'll return to the Playback menu; if you chose No, you'll be taken back to the selection screen to mark/unmark images.

5. **Exit.** To back out of the selection screen, press the MENU button or tap the Return icon.

■ **Select Date.** Highlight any of the available dates that have pictures, and press the multi selector right button to add a check mark to that date. Press the Zoom Out/Thumbnail button to view/confirm that the images for the date you've marked are those you want to delete, and press the button again to return to the Select Date screen. When you're finished choosing dates, press OK to delete the images from the confirmation screen.

■ **All.** This removes all the "unprotected" images from your memory card. Keep in mind that Format is a faster way to remove images, but, unlike All, it deletes those marked as Protected as well.

Playback Folder

Options: D5500, All, Current

My preference: N/A

Your Nikon D5500 will create folders on your memory card to store the images that it creates. It assigns the first folder a number, like 100D5500, and when that folder fills with 999 images, the camera automatically creates a new folder numbered one higher, such as 101D5500. If you use the same memory card in another camera, that camera will also create its own folder. Thus you can end up with several folders on the same memory card, until you eventually reformat the card and folder creation starts anew.

This menu item allows you to choose which folders are accessed when displaying images using the D5500's Playback facility. Your choices are as follows:

- **D5500.** If you use the same memory card in more than one camera, each additional camera will automatically create a new folder for its images only. The D5500 is often able to display these "foreign" images with no problem, especially if they were created by another Nikon camera. If you choose this entry, the D5500 will play back *only* images created by your D5500, and ignore those created by other cameras. If you find the other images don't display properly, or you just prefer to skip over them, select this entry or Current.

- **Current.** The D5500 will display only images in the current folder. For example, if you have been shooting heavily at an event and have already accumulated more than 999 shots in one folder and the D5500 has created a new folder for the overflow, you'd use this setting to view only the most recent photos, which reside in the current folder. You can change the current folder to any other folder on your memory card using the Active Folder option in the Shooting menu.

- **All.** All folders containing images that the D5500 can read will be accessed, regardless of which camera created them. You might want to use this setting if you swap memory cards among several cameras and want to be able to review all the photos (especially when considering reformatting the memory card). You will be able to view images even if they were created by a non-Nikon camera if those images conform to the Design Rule for Camera File System (DCF) specifications.

Playback Display Options

Options: None (image only), Highlights, RGB Histogram, Shooting Data, Overview

My preference: I prefer to enable all available information screens.

This menu item helps you reduce/increase the color LCD monitor clutter on playback by specifying which information and screens will be available. To activate or deactivate an info option, scroll to that option and press the right multi selector button or OK button to add a check mark to the box next to that item. Press the right button or OK button to unmark an item that has previously been checked. **Important:** when you're finished, you must scroll up to Done and press OK or the right multi selector button to confirm your choices. Exiting the Display Mode menu any other way will cause any changes you may have made to be ignored. Your info options include:

- **None.** This choice does *not* mean that all information will be hidden. (To do that, you'd need to uncheck all the boxes on this screen.) When you select this option, a playback screen with no shooting information will be shown in the cycle displayed when you press the up/down multi selector buttons.

- **Highlights.** When enabled, overexposed highlight areas in your image will blink with a black border during picture review. That's your cue to consider using exposure compensation to reduce exposure, unless a minus-EV setting will cause loss of shadow detail that you want to preserve.

- **RGB Histogram.** Displays both luminance (brightness) and RGB histograms on a screen that can be displayed using the up/down multi selector buttons, as shown in Chapter 2.

- **Shooting Data.** Activates the three pages of shooting data shown in Chapter 2. (Flip back if you need a refresher.)

- **Overview.** Marking this enables the Overview screen shown in Chapter 2.

Image Review

Options: On (default), Off

My preference: N/A

While instant review is useful, sometimes it's a better idea to *not* automatically review your shots in order to conserve battery power, speed up, or simplify operations. This menu operation allows you to choose which mode to use:

- **On.** Image review is automatic after every shot is taken.

- **Off.** Images are displayed only when you press the Playback button.

Auto Image Rotation

Options: On (default), Off

My preference: On

Turning this setting On tells the Nikon D5500 to include camera orientation information in the image file. The orientation can be read by many software applications, including Adobe Photoshop, Nikon ViewNX, and Capture NX, as well as the Rotate Tall setting in the Playback menu. Turn this feature Off, and none of the software applications or Playback's Rotate Tall will be able to determine the correct orientation for the image. Nikon notes that only the first image's orientation is used when shooting continuous bursts; subsequent photos will be assigned the same orientation, even if you rotate the camera during the sequence (which is something I have been known to do myself when shooting sports like basketball).

Rotate Tall

Options: On (default), Off

My preference: On

The D5500's internal directional sensor can detect whether the camera was rotated when the photo was taken and embed this information in the image file itself. It can be used by the D5500 to automatically rotate images when they are displayed on the camera's LCD monitor (providing a smaller image), or you can ignore the data and let the images display in non-rotated fashion (so you have to rotate the camera to view them in their larger, full-screen orientation). Your image-editing application can also use the embedded file data to automatically rotate images on your computer screen.

This works *only* if you've told the D5500 to place orientation information in the image file so it can be retrieved when the image is displayed. You must set Auto Image Rotation to On in the Setup menu, as described in Chapter 4. Then, both your D5500 and your image editor can rotate the images for you as the files are displayed.

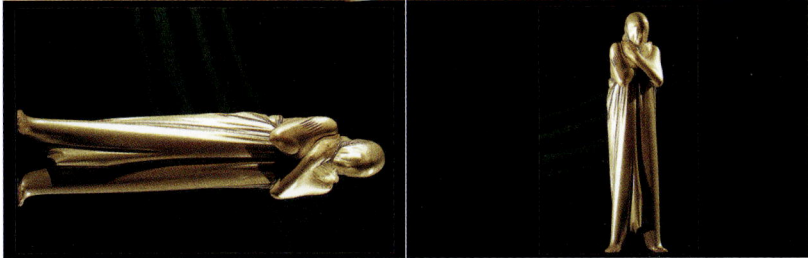

Figure 3.3 With Rotate Tall turned off, vertical images appear large on the LCD monitor, but you must turn the camera to view them upright. With Rotate Tall turned on, vertical images are shown in a smaller size, but oriented for viewing without turning the camera.

This menu choice deals only with whether the image should be rotated when displayed on the *camera LCD monitor*. When Rotate Tall is turned off, the Nikon D5500 does not rotate pictures taken in vertical orientation. The image is large on your LCD monitor screen, but you must rotate the camera to view it upright. When Rotate Tall is turned on, the D5500 rotates pictures taken in vertical orientation on the LCD monitor screen so you don't have to turn the camera to view them comfortably. However, this orientation also means that the longest dimension of the image is shown using the shortest dimension of the LCD monitor, so the picture is reduced in size. (See Figure 3.3.)

Slide Show

Options: Start, Frame Interval (default 2 seconds)

My preference: N/A

The D5500's Slide Show feature is a convenient way to review images in the current playback folder one after another, without the need to manually switch between them. To activate, just choose Start from this entry in the Playback menu. If you like, you can choose Frame Interval before commencing the show in order to select an interval of 2, 3, 5, or 10 seconds between "slides."

During playback, you can press the OK button to pause the "slide show" (in case you want to examine an image more closely). When the show is paused, a menu pops up, as shown in Figure 3.4, with choices to restart the show (by pressing the OK button again); change the interval between frames; or to exit the show entirely.

As the images are displayed, press the up/down multi selector buttons to change the amount of information presented on the screen with each image. For example, you might want to review a set of images and the settings used to shoot them. At any time during the show, press the up/down buttons until the informational screen you want is overlaid on the images.

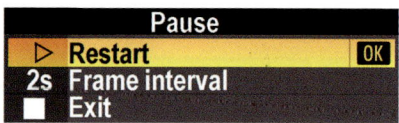

Figure 3.4
Press the OK button to pause the slide show, change the interval between slides, or to exit the presentation.

As the slide show progresses, you can press the left/right multi selector buttons to move back to a previous frame or jump ahead to the next one. The slide show will then proceed as before. Press the MENU button to exit the slide show and return to the menu, or the Playback button to exit the menu system totally. As always, while reviewing images you can tap the MENU button to exit the show and return to the menus, or tap the shutter release button if you want to remove everything from the screen and return to shooting mode.

At the end of the slide show, as when you've paused it, you'll be offered the choice of restarting the sequence, changing the frame interval, or exiting the slide show feature completely.

DPOF Print Order

Options: Select/Set, Deselect All

My preference: N/A

You can print directly from your camera to a printer compatible with a specification called *PictBridge*. You can mark images in the camera, and then remove your memory card and hand it to your retailer for printing in their lab or in-store printing machine, or insert the card into a stand-alone picture kiosk and make prints yourself. This menu lets you specify which photos you want printed, and how many copies you'd like of each picture. If you're taking photos in PSAM modes with the expectation of printing them through a direct USB connection, set Color Space to sRGB for best results, in the Shooting menu, described next.

When you choose this menu item, you're presented with a set of screens that look very much like the Delete Photos screens described earlier, only you're selecting pictures for printing rather than deleting them. The first screen you see when you choose Print Set (DPOF) asks if you'd like to Select/Set pictures for printing, or Deselect All? images that have already been marked. Choose Select/Set to choose photos and specify how many prints of each you'd like (see Figure 3.5). Choose Deselect All? to cancel any existing print order and start over.

1. **Scroll.** Use the multi selector cursor keys to scroll among the available images. You can also scroll by sliding a finger up or down the touch screen and tapping on an image to highlight it.

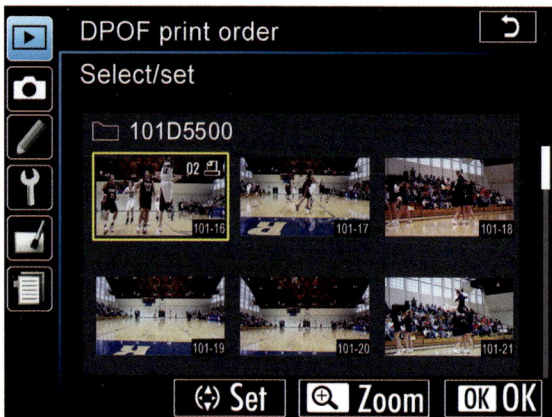

Figure 3.5
Select images for printing.

2. **Zoom in.** When you highlight an image you think you might like to print, press the Zoom In button to temporarily enlarge that image so you can evaluate it further. When you release the Zoom In button, the selection screen returns. You can also zoom in by tapping the Zoom icon at the bottom of the screen; however, to zoom back out you must either tap the Return icon in the upper-right corner, or press the OK button. I find it's much easier to simply press and release the Zoom In button rather than resort to the touch screen.

3. **Mark images.** To mark an image for printing, press the multi selector up button to choose the number of prints you want, up to 99 per image. To deselect or decrease the number of prints, press the multi selector down button. You can also increment the number of prints by tapping a thumbnail on the touch screen or the Set icon, but you still must use the down button to decrement.

4. **Confirm.** When you've finished marking images to print, press OK or tap the OK icon at the bottom of the screen. A final screen will appear in which you can request a data imprint (shutter speed and aperture) or imprint date (the date the photos were taken). Select one or both of these options, if desired, and press the left/right buttons to mark or tap the box or unmark the check boxes. When a box is marked, the imprint information for that option will be included on *all* prints in the print order.

Rating

Options: Set one to five stars, plus delete marker

My preference: N/A

Allows applying a star rating from one to five stars for individual images. Choose this menu item and the image selection window will appear. You can use the left/right directional buttons to scroll among your images to highlight one you want to rate. To view a highlighted image full frame, press and hold the Zoom In button. Rate a highlighted image using the up/down buttons to apply a rating from zero to five stars, or tap the thumbnail one to five times. Press the down button to decrement stars, or to select the Trash icon to mark the picture for later deletion. Ratings cannot be applied to protected images. Press OK or tap Return to confirm and exit.

Images can also be rated during playback. When an image is shown on the screen as you review it, press the *i* button to show playback options (Rating, Retouch, Select to Send to Smart Device/Deselect). Choose Rating, and then use the controls to apply a rating as described above. Press OK to confirm and exit.

This capability is much more versatile than you might think. The stars don't have to relate to relative image quality. You can invent any other "code" you might like to apply. For example, if you like, one star can represent photos containing animals; two stars pictures with family members; three stars photos of landscapes; and so forth. Then, with the ratings applied, you can quickly access particular types of pictures.

Select To Send to Smart Device

Options: Choose images to transfer

My preference: N/A

Allows selected photos (but not movies) to be uploaded to a smart device. Choose this menu item and the familiar image selection window will appear. You can use the left/right directional buttons to scroll among your images to highlight one you want to select. To view a highlighted image full frame, press and hold the Zoom In button. Select a highlighted image by pressing the Zoom Out button. Selected photos are marked with a double-headed arrow icon. You can select multiple images. When finished, press OK to confirm and exit.

Images can also be selected during playback. When an image is shown on the screen as you review it, press the *i* button to show playback options (Rating, Retouch, Select to Send to Smart Device/Deselect). Choose Select to Send to Smart Device/Deselect, and press OK or tap Return to confirm.

Shooting Menu Options

These settings are likely to be the most common settings changes you make. The first eight choices are shown in Figure 3.6.

- Reset Shooting Menu
- Storage Folder
- File Naming
- Image Quality
- Image Size
- NEF (RAW) Recording
- ISO Sensitivity Settings
- White Balance
- Set Picture Control
- Manage Picture Control

- Color Space
- Active D-Lighting
- HDR (High Dynamic Range)
- Release Mode
- Long Exp. NR
- High ISO NR
- Vignette Control
- Auto Distortion Control
- Interval Timer Shooting
- Movie Settings

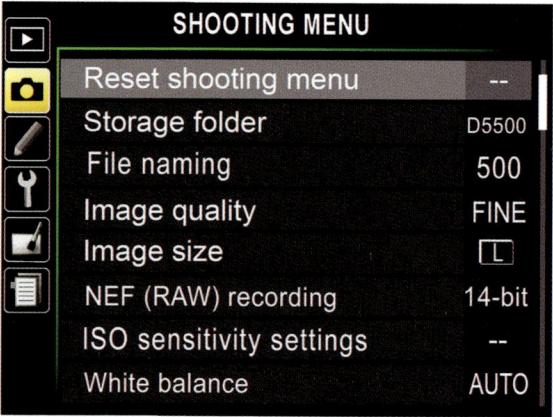

Figure 3.6
This is the first page of the Shooting menu.

Reset Shooting Menu

Options: None

My preference: N/A

If you select Yes, the Shooting menu settings shown in Table 3.1 will be set to their default values. It has no effect on the settings in other menus, or any of the other camera settings. You'd want to use this Reset option when you've made a bunch of changes (say, while playing around with them as you read this chapter), and now want to put them back to the factory defaults.

Storage Folder

Options: Select Folder by Number, Select Folder from List

My preference: N/A

If you want to store images in a folder other than the one created and selected by the Nikon D5500, you can switch among available folders on your memory card, or create your own folder. Any folders you create will be deleted when you reformat your memory card.

To change the currently active folder:

1. **Access active folder entry.** Choose Storage Folder in the Shooting menu, and press the right multi selector button.
2. **Choose selection method.** Highlight either Select Folder by Number or Select Folder from List (to choose a folder that you know already exists). Press the right directional button or tap the touch screen to confirm your choice. One of two screens appears. Perform the tasks in *either* Step 3 or Step 4.
3. **Select Folder by Number.** If you've chosen this option, a screen appears with three digits representing the possible folder numbers from 100 to 999. Use the left/right multi selector buttons or touch controls to move between the digits, and the up/down controls to increase or decrease the value of the digit. If a folder already exists with the number you dial in, an icon appears showing the folder is empty, partially full, or it has 999 images or a picture numbered 9999 (and can contain no more images). Press OK to create the new folder and make it the active folder. You'd want to use this option to create a new folder *or* when you don't know whether a folder by a particular number already exists. If a folder with that number already resides on the memory card, you can use it (if it is not full); if it doesn't exist, you can create it.

Table 3.1 Default Shooting Menu Values

Function	Default Value
Reset Shooting Menu	None
Storage Folder	None
File Naming	DSC
Image Quality	JPEG Normal
Image Size	Large
NEF (Raw) Recording	14 bit
ISO Sensitivity Settings	
P, S, A, M modes	100
Other exposure modes	Auto
Auto ISO sensitivity control	Off
White Balance	Auto
Fluorescent	Cool-white
Set Picture Control	Standard
Manage Picture Control	None
Color Space	sRGB
Active D-Lighting	Auto
HDR (high dynamic range)	Off
Release Mode	
Sports, Pets	Continuous H
Other modes	Single Frame
Long Exposure Noise Reduction	Off
High ISO Noise Reduction	Normal
Vignette Control	Normal
Auto Distortion Control	Off
Interval Timer Shooting	
Start Options	Now
Interval	1 min.
Number of Times	1
Exposure Smoothing	Off
Movie Settings	
Frame Size/Frame Rate	1920 × 1080/60i
Movie Quality	Normal
Microphone	Auto Sensitivity
Wind Noise Reduction	Off
Manual Movie Settings	Off

4. **Select Folder from List.** From among the available folders shown, scroll to the one that you want to become active for image storage and playback. This feature is handy when you want to display a slide show located in a particular folder. Use this option if you know that the folder you want to use already resides on the memory card. Press OK to confirm your choice and make the folder active.

Entering Text on the Nikon D5500

Now is a good time to master text entry, because you can use it to enter comments, rename folders, and perform other functions. The Nikon D5500 uses a fairly standardized text entry screen to name files and Picture Controls, create new folder names, and enter image comments and other text. You'll be using text entry with other functions that I'll describe later in this book. The screen looks like the one shown in Figure 3.7, with some variations (for example, some functions have a less diverse character set, or offer more or fewer spaces for your entries). To select your file name prefix, first select File Naming, then use the right multi selector button or touch controls to reveal the text entry screen. After that, you can use the multi selector navigational buttons or touch controls to scroll around within the array of alphanumerics, and enter your text. This is one function that really takes advantage of the touch screen, because you can "type" the characters you want to use rather than tediously scroll among the rows and columns with the directional buttons.

■ **Highlight a character.** Tap the character you want to enter on the touch screen (or, if you're wearing gloves, use the multi selector keys to scroll around within the array of characters).

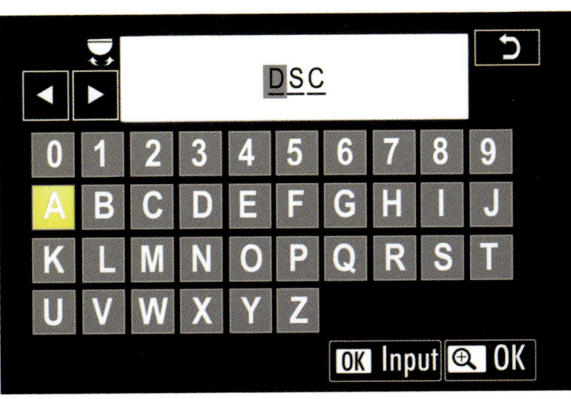

Figure 3.7
Use this D5500 screen to enter text.

- **Insert highlighted character.** Press the multi selector center OK button (or tap the OK Input icon) to insert the highlighted character. The cursor will move one place to the right to accept the next character.

- **Non-destructively backspace.** Use the command dial or the left/right arrows in the upper-left corner of the display to move the cursor within the naming field. This allows you to backspace and replace a character without disturbing the others you've entered.

- **Confirm your entry.** When you're finished entering text, press the Zoom In button or tap Return to confirm your entry, then tap the shutter release to exit the menu system.

File Naming

Options: DSC (default), Three characters

My preference: 550

The D5500, like other cameras in the Nikon product line, automatically applies a name like _DSC0001.jpg or DSC_0001.nef to your image files as they are created. You can use this menu option to change the names applied to your photos, but only within certain strict limitations. In practice, you can change only three of the eight characters, the *DSC* portion of the file name. The other five are mandated either by the Design Rule for Camera File System (DCF) specification that all digital camera makers adhere to or to industry conventions.

Image Quality

Options: NEF (RAW) + JPEG Fine, NEF (RAW) + JPEG Normal, NEF (RAW) + JPEG Basic, NEF (RAW), JPEG Fine, JPEG Normal (Default), JPEG Basic

My preference: NEF (RAW) + JPEG Fine. I use 64GB and 128GB memory cards and have multiple 3TB hard drives on my computer, so saving storage space is not a concern.

You can choose the image quality settings used by the D5500 to store its files. Just use the information edit screen. You can also use this menu option (see Figure 3.8) and the next one, if you prefer. You have two choices to make:

- **Level of JPEG compression.** Compacting images reduces the quality a little, so you're offered your choice of Fine (a 1:4 reduction), Normal (1:8 reduction), and Basic (1:16 reduction) compression.

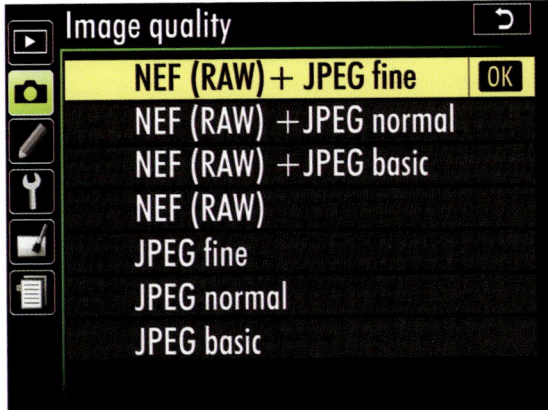

Figure 3.8
Choose image quality.

- **JPEG, RAW, or both.** You can elect to store only Fine, Normal, or Basic JPEG versions of the images you shoot, or you can save your photos as RAW images, which Nikon calls NEF, for Nikon Electronic Format files. RAW images consume more than twice as much space on your memory card. Or, you can store both RAW and a JPEG Fine, Normal, or Basic file at once as you shoot.

Image Size

Options: Large (default), Medium, Small

My preference: Large

The next menu command in the Shooting menu lets you select the resolution, or number of pixels, captured as you shoot with your Nikon D5500. Your choices range from Large (L—6000 × 4000 pixels, 24 megapixels), Medium (M—4496 × 3000 pixels, 13 megapixels), and Small (S—2992 × 2000 pixels, 6.0 megapixels). There are no additional options available from the Image Size menu screen.

NEF (RAW) Recording

Options: 12 bit, 14 bit (default)

My preference: 14 bit. I like all the information I can get for my RAW files.

Here you can choose whether your images are stored using 12-bit or 14-bit depth. The default value for color depth (14 bit) works best for most situations, but there are times when you might want to use 12-bit RAW storage, perhaps to save a little memory card space. You should probably leave your D5500 set for 14-bit color, which will give you a possible 4,398,046,391,104 (4.4 trillion) different colors in your captured image. By comparison, 12-bit color offers a total of 68,719,476,736 (68.7 billion) colors.

The bottom line is that the 14-bit setting improves your chances that the colors available for storing your image will correspond to the actual colors in your scene, but with a slight penalty in file size. It's especially useful when you're exposing images that will be combined using HDR (high dynamic range) software later on. In that case, you can definitely gain some extra exposure "headroom" using 14-bit processing. In either case, an image editor will reduce the actual number of colors in your file from billions and trillions down to mere millions—16.8 million in the final 8-bit image file produced by Photoshop, Photoshop Elements, or other editors.

ISO Sensitivity Settings

Options: ISO Sensitivity (default, Off), Auto ISO Sensitivity Control, Maximum Sensitivity, and Minimum Shutter Speed

My preference: I leave Auto ISO off most of the time, and prefer to set my own ISO values so there are no noise-filled "surprises" later on.

This menu entry has four parts: ISO Sensitivity, Auto ISO Sensitivity Control, Maximum Sensitivity, and Minimum Shutter Speed. You can select a specific ISO setting, or control how the D5500 chooses an ISO setting automatically. The Auto ISO Sensitivity Control menu entry lets you specify how and when the D5500 will adjust the ISO value for you automatically under certain conditions.

When Auto ISO is activated, the camera can bump up the ISO sensitivity, if necessary, whenever an optimal exposure cannot be achieved at the current ISO setting. Here are the important considerations to keep in mind when using the options available for this feature:

- **ISO Sensitivity.** This option allows you to choose specific ISO settings in one-third stop increments, from ISO 100 (the default) though ISO 25600.
- **Auto ISO Sensitivity.** Set ISO Sensitivity Auto Control to Off (the default), and the ISO setting will not budge from whatever value you have specified.
- **Maximum Sensitivity.** Use this parameter, available only when Auto ISO Sensitivity is on, to indicate the highest ISO setting you're comfortable having the D5500 set on its own. You can choose from ISO 400, 800, 1600, 3200, 6400, 12800, and 25600 as the max ISO setting the camera

will use. Use a low number if you'd rather not take any photos at a high ISO without manually setting that value yourself. Dial in a higher ISO number if getting the photo at any sensitivity setting is more important than worrying about noise.

■ **Minimum Shutter Speed.** This setting, accessible when Auto ISO Sensitivity is on, allows you to tell the D5500 how slow the shutter speed must be before the ISO boost kicks in, within the range 1 second to 1/2,000th second, plus Auto. The default value is 1/30th second, because for most shooters in most situations, any shutter speed longer than 1/30th second is to be avoided, unless you're using a tripod, monopod, or looking for a special effect. When the shutter speed is faster than the minimum you enter, Auto ISO will not take effect.

White Balance

Options: Auto (default), Incandescent, Fluorescent (Sodium Vapor, Warm-White, White, Cool-White, Day White, Daylight, High Temp. Mercury-Vapor), Direct Sunlight, Flash, Cloudy, Shade, Preset Manual

My preference: Auto

When you select the White Balance entry on the Shooting menu, you'll see an array of choices like those shown at left in Figure 3.9. (One additional choice, Preset Manual, is not visible until you scroll down to it.) If you choose Fluorescent, you'll be taken to another screen that presents seven different types of lamps, from sodium-vapor through warm-white fluorescent down to high-temperature mercury-vapor. If you know the exact type of non-incandescent lighting being used, you can select it, or settle on a likely compromise.

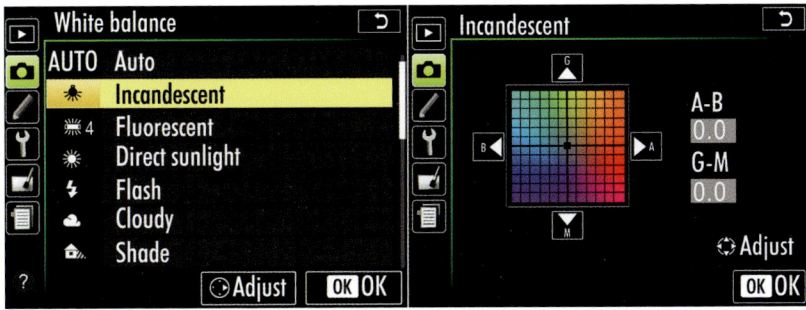

Figure 3.9 The White Balance menu has predefined values, plus the option of setting a preset you measure yourself (left). Specific white balance settings can be fine-tuned by changing their bias in the amber/blue, magenta/green directions—or along both axes simultaneously (right).

For all other settings (Auto, Incandescent, Direct Sunlight, Flash, Cloudy, or Shade), highlight the white balance option you want, then press the multi selector right button (or press OK) to view the fine-tuning screen shown at right in Figure 3.9 (and which uses the Incandescent setting as an example). The screen shows a grid with two axes, a blue/amber axis extending left/right, and a green/magenta axis extending up and down the grid. By default, the grid's cursor is positioned in the middle, and a readout to the right of the grid shows the cursor's coordinates on the A-B axis (yes, I know the display has the end points reversed) and G-M axis at 0,0.

You can use the multi selector's up/down and right/left buttons to move the cursor to any coordinate in the grid, thereby biasing the white balance in the direction(s) you choose. The amber-blue axis makes the image warmer or colder (but not actually yellow or blue). Similarly, the green-magenta axis preserves all the colors in the original image, but gives them a tinge biased toward green or magenta. Each increment equals about five mired units, but you should know that mired values aren't linear; five mireds at 2,500K produces a much stronger effect than five mireds at 6,000K. If you really want to fine-tune your color balance, you're better off experimenting and evaluating the results of a particular change.

Using Preset Manual White Balance

If automatic white balance or one of the predefined settings available aren't suitable, you can set a custom white balance using the Preset Manual menu option. You can apply the white balance from a scene, either by shooting a new picture on the spot and using the resulting white balance (Measure) or using an image you have already shot (Use Photo). To perform direct measurement from your current scene using a reference object (preferably a neutral gray or white object), follow these steps:

1. **Position reference subject.** Place the neutral reference under the lighting you want to measure.
2. **Change to Preset Manual white balance.** Access the White Balance menu entry, scroll down to Preset Manual, and press the right multi selector button. There, you'll see a screen with a choice of Measure or Use Photo.
3. **Highlight Measure.** Press OK to confirm.
4. **Overwrite existing data.** A screen appears asking whether you want to overwrite the existing Preset Manual value. Highlight Yes and press OK to proceed.

5. **Take photo.** Take a picture of your neutral reference subject.

6. **Confirm successful capture of white balance.** If the camera successfully measured white balance, "Gd" will appear in the bottom line of the viewfinder, and "Data Acquired" will appear on the shooting information screen on the LCD monitor. Otherwise, you'll see "no Gd" on the viewfinder. White balance measurement can fail when the reference object is too brightly or poorly illuminated. In that case, repeat steps 2 to 5 until the measurement is successful.

7. **Use captured white balance.** You can immediately begin taking pictures using the captured white balance, until you switch to one of the other white balance settings, such as Tungsten or Fluorescent. The next time you switch to Preset Manual, the white balance you just captured will be used again.

Storing and Retrieving White Balance Settings

If you want to use an existing photo, choose Use Photo, and a screen will appear offering to use the most recently taken image, or you can Select Image from a folder of your choice, accessing the standard D5500 selection screen similar to the ones shown previously.

Set Picture Control

Options: Standard (default), Neutral, Vivid, Monochrome, Portrait, Landscape, Flat, plus 9 user-definable controls

My preference: Standard for general shooting; Flat when I want JPEGs with maximum dynamic range. However, I'll always have my RAW files for serious tweaking.

This is the first entry in the second page of the Shooting menu (see Figure 3.10). Nikon provides seven predefined styles (Standard, Neutral, Vivid, Monochrome, Portrait, Landscape, and Flat). However, you can *edit* the settings of any of those styles (but not rename them) so they better suit your taste. The D5500 also offers nine user-definable Picture Control styles (described next) that you can edit to your heart's content and assign descriptive names. You can copy these styles to a memory card, edit them on your computer, and reload them into your camera at any time. So, effectively, you can have a lot more than nine custom Picture Control styles available: the nine in your camera, as well as a virtually unlimited library of user-defined styles that you have stored on memory cards. These Picture Controls are available when you're using PSAM exposure modes. In other modes, the camera selects a Picture Control automatically.

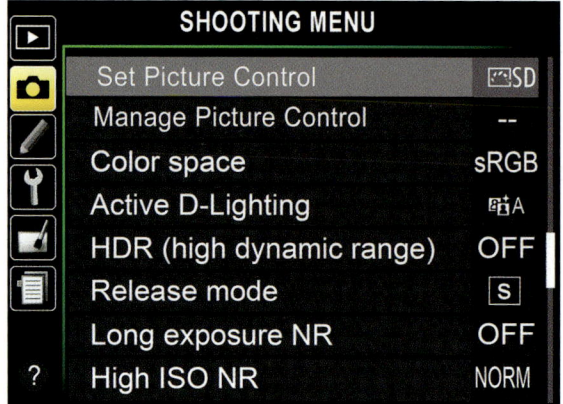

Figure 3.10
The second page of
the Shooting menu.

The Flat control is a relatively new Picture Control in the Nikon world, and ideal for images and video clips that will be retouched, as it provides a much greater dynamic range with detailed shadows and highlights, so you can tweak the images extensively if necessary. Flat is especially popular among video shooters because of this deeper range.

Nikon insists that these styles have been standardized to the extent that if you re-use a style created for one camera (say, your D5500) and load it into a different compatible camera (such as a Nikon D4s), you'll get substantially the same rendition, so you can use a style created by anyone else that you have Googled and downloaded from the Internet.

Using and managing Picture Control styles is accomplished using two different menu entries, Set Picture Control, which allows you to choose an existing style and to edit the predefined styles that Nikon provides, and Manage Picture Control, which gives you the capability of creating and editing user-defined styles.

Choosing a Picture Control Style

To choose from one of the predefined styles or select a user-defined style (numbered C-1 to C-9), follow these steps:

1. **Choose Set Picture Control.** This option is located in the Shooting menu. The screen shown in Figure 3.11 appears. Note that Picture Controls that have been modified from their standard settings have an asterisk next to their name.

2. **Select style.** Scroll down to the Picture Control you'd like to use.

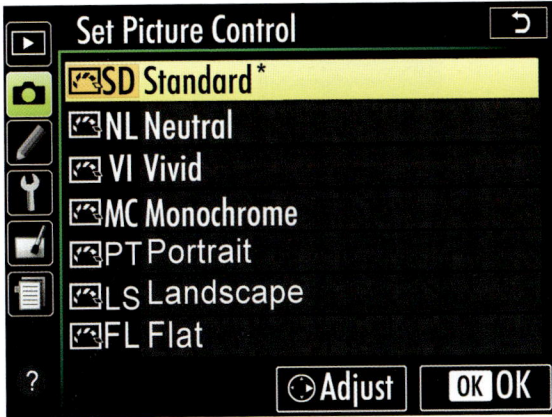

Figure 3.11
You can choose from the predefined Picture Controls.

3. **Activate Picture Control.** Press OK to activate the highlighted style. (Although you can usually select a menu item by pressing the multi selector right button, in this case, that button activates editing instead.)

4. **Exit menu.** Press the MENU button or tap the shutter release to exit the menu system.

Editing a Picture Control Style

You can change the parameters of any of Nikon's predefined Picture Controls. You are given the choice of using the quick adjust/fine-tune facility to modify a Picture Control with a few sliders, or to view the relationship of your Picture Controls on a grid. To make quick adjustments to any Picture Control except the Monochrome style, follow these steps:

1. **Access menu.** Choose Set Picture Control from the Shooting menu.

2. **Select style.** Scroll down to the Picture Control you'd like to edit.

3. **Access adjustment screen.** Press the multi selector right button to produce the adjustment screen shown in Figure 3.12.

4. **Make fast changes.** Use the Quick Adjust slider to exaggerate the attributes of the Standard or Vivid styles (Quick Adjustments are not available with other styles).

5. **Change other attributes.** Scroll down to the Sharpening, Clarity, Contrast, Brightness, Saturation, and Hue sliders, then use the left/right buttons to decrease or increase the effects, or tap an adjustment to produce a screen with more detailed sliders. A line will appear under the original setting in the slider whenever you've made a change from the

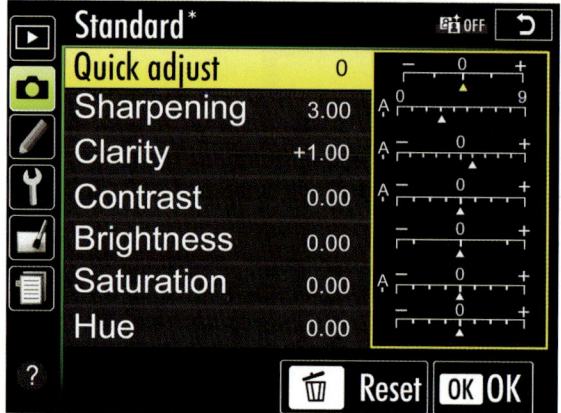

Figure 3.12

Sliders can be used to make quick adjustments to your Picture Control styles.

defaults. **Note:** You can't adjust contrast and brightness when Active D-Lighting (discussed later in this chapter) is active. Turn it off to make those Picture Control adjustments. An icon at the upper right of the screen shows whether Active D-Lighting is on or off.

6. **Or use auto adjustments.** Instead of making changes with the slider's scale, you can move the cursor to the far left and choose A (for auto) instead when working with the Sharpening, Contrast, and Saturation sliders. The D5500 will adjust these parameters automatically, depending on the type of scene it detects.

7. **To Reset Values.** Press the Trash button to reset the values to their defaults.

8. **Confirm changes.** Press/tap OK when you're finished making adjustments.

Editing the Monochrome style is similar, except that the parameters are Sharpening, Contrast, Brightness, Filter Effects (Yellow, Orange, Red, Green, or None), as well as toning effects (black-and-white, plus seven levels of Sepia, Cyanotype, Red, Yellow, Green, Blue Green, Blue, Purple Blue, and Red Purple). (Keep in mind that once you've taken a JPEG photo using a Monochrome style, you can't convert the image back to full color. Shoot using RAW+JPEG, and you'll get a monochrome JPEG, plus the RAW file that retains all the color information.) Filter Effects produce a grayscale image that looks as if it were shot with black-and-white film using a color filter on the lens (no color tone is produced). (See Figure 3.13.) Toning Effects give you a tinted monochrome filter in various colors. (See Figure 3.14.)

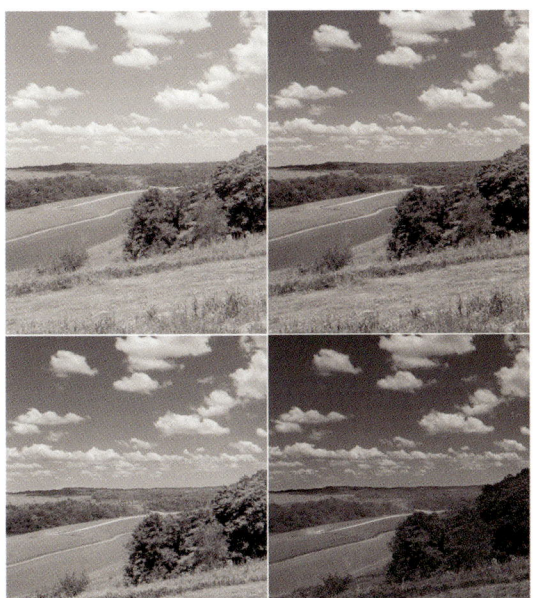

Figure 3.13
No filter (upper left); Yellow filter (upper right); Green filter (lower left); and Red filter (lower right).

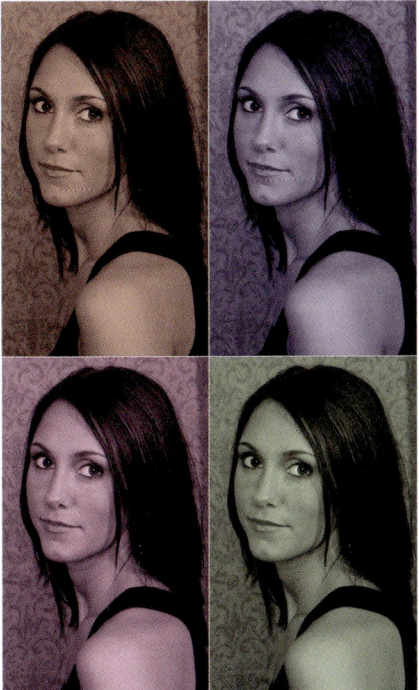

Figure 3.14
Toning effects: Sepia (upper left); Purple Blue (upper right); Red Purple (lower left); and Green (lower right).

Manage Picture Control

Options: Save/Edit, Rename, Delete, Load/Save

My preference: N/A

The Manage Picture Control menu entry can be used to create new styles, edit existing styles, rename or delete styles, and store/retrieve styles from the memory card.

- **Make a copy.** Choose Save/Edit, select from the list of available Picture Controls, and press OK to store that style in one of the user-defined slots C-1 to C-9.

- **Save an edited copy.** Choose Save/Edit, select from the list of available Picture Controls, and then press the multi selector right button to edit the style, as described in the previous section. Press OK when finished editing, and then save the modified style in one of the user-defined slots C-1 to C-9.

- **Rename a style.** Choose Rename, select from the list of user-defined Picture Controls (you cannot rename the default styles), and then enter the text used as the new label for the style, using the standard D5500 text entry screen like those shown earlier in this chapter.

- **Remove a style.** Select Delete, choose from the list of user-defined Picture Controls (you can't remove one of the default styles), press the multi selector right button, then highlight Yes in the screen that follows, and press OK to remove that Picture Control.

- **Store/retrieve style on card.** Choose Load/Save, then select Copy to Camera to locate a Picture Control on your memory card and copy it to the D5500; Delete from Card to select a Picture Control on your memory card and remove it; or Copy to Card to duplicate a style currently in your camera onto the memory card.

Color Space

Options: sRGB (default), Adobe RGB

My preference: sRGB

The Nikon D5500's Color Space option gives you two different color spaces: Adobe RGB (because it was developed by Adobe Systems in 1998), and sRGB (supposedly because it is the *standard* RGB color space). Regardless of which color space is used by the D5500, you end up with some combination of 16.8 million different colors that can be seen in your photograph.

Adobe RGB is an expanded color space useful for commercial and professional printing, and it can reproduce a wider range of colors. However, as an advanced user, you don't need to automatically "upgrade" your D5500 to Adobe RGB, because images tend to look less saturated on your monitor and, it is likely, significantly different from what you will get if you output the photo to your personal inkjet. (You can *profile* your monitor for the Adobe RGB color space to improve your on-screen rendition.) While both Adobe RGB and sRGB can reproduce the exact same 16.8 million absolute colors, Adobe RGB spreads those colors over a larger portion of the visible spectrum.

The sRGB space is recommended for images that will be output locally on the user's own printer, as it matches that of the typical inkjet printer fairly closely. It is well suited for the range of colors that can be displayed on a computer screen and viewed over the Internet. If you plan to take your image file to a retailer's kiosk for printing, sRGB is your best choice, because those automated output devices are calibrated for the sRGB color space that consumers use. If you shoot RAW or RAW+JPEG, with the camera set to one color space, you can extract the other from the RAW file at any time.

Active D-Lighting

Options: Auto (default), Extra High, High, Normal, Low, Off

My preference: Off. I save this feature for high-contrast scenes that really need it; Auto sometimes kicks in when I don't really want to use it.

D-Lighting is a feature that improves the rendition of detail in highlights and shadows when you're photographing high-contrast scenes (those that have dramatic differences between the brightest areas and the darkest areas that hold detail). Unlike the post-shot D-Lighting feature found in the Retouch menu, Active D-Lighting can be applied to your pictures *while you are actually taking the photo.*

For best results, use your D5500's Matrix metering mode, so the Active D-Lighting feature can work with a full range of exposure information from multiple points in the image. Active D-Lighting works its magic by subtly *underexposing* your image so that details in the highlights (which would normally be overexposed and become featureless white pixels) are not lost. At the same time, it adjusts the values of pixels located in midtone and shadow areas so they don't become too dark because of the underexposure. Highlight tones will be preserved, while shadows will eventually be allowed to go dark more readily. Bright beach or snow scenes, especially those with few shadows (think high noon, when the shadows are smaller), can benefit from using Active

D-Lighting. You have six choices: Auto, Extra High, High, Normal, Low, and Off. You may need to experiment with the feature a little to discover how much D-Lighting you can apply to a high-contrast image before the shadows start to darken objectionably. Note that when this feature is activated, brightness and contrast Picture Control settings cannot be changed.

HDR (High Dynamic Range)

Options: Auto, Extra High, High, Normal, Low, Off (default)

My preference: Off. Most of my HDR work is done using bracketed exposures.

When activated, the D5500's in-camera HDR will capture two exposures, which can be separated by no more than three stops' worth of exposure. The HDR entry has one set of options: you can choose Auto to allow the camera to decide how much HDR correction to apply; Off, to disable the feature; or select a level, using Low, Normal, High, or Extra High. This feature is not available if NEF or NEF+JPEG settings are selected.

Release Mode

Options: Single Frame, Continuous L, Continuous H, Self-Timer, Quiet Shutter Release, 2s Delayed Remote, Quick Response Remote

My preference: N/A

This entry duplicates the release mode settings available when the release mode/drive button is pressed. You can choose:

- **Single frame.** In single-shot mode, the D5500 takes one picture each time you press the shutter release button down all the way.

- **Continuous L/Continuous H.** These modes fire off shots at up to 3 and 5 frames per second, respectively.

- **Self-timer.** You can use the self-timer as a replacement for a remote release, to reduce the effects of camera/user shake when the D5500 is mounted on a tripod or, say, set on a firm surface, or when you want to get in the picture yourself. Use Custom Setting c3 to specify delays of 2, 5, 10, or 20 seconds. You can also specify the number of shots taken at the end of the elapsed period, and the interval between those shots.

- **Quiet shutter release.** This setting, marked with a Q symbol, activates the D5500's "quiet mode," which silences the camera's beep noise during autofocus, reduces the sound the mirror makes when it flips back down, and delays that "noise" until you release the shutter button.

■ **2s Delayed Remote/Quick Response Remote (ML-L3).** If you use the ML-L3 infrared remote, you'll need to change the release mode to either of these two settings: Delayed Remote (shutter releases two seconds after you press the button on the ML-L3 IR remote) or Quick Response Remote (the shutter trips immediately when the button is pressed). Once you've selected either of these two release modes, the camera then "looks" for the remote signal for a period of time you specify using Custom Setting c4 (select from 1, 5, 10, or 15 minutes).

Long Exp. NR

Options: Off (default), On

My preference: Off. The process takes extra time, and I find that noise reduction can be better applied in an image editor or RAW converter, which allow you to fine-tune the amount of reduction.

Visual noise is that awful graininess caused by long exposures and high ISO settings, and which shows up as multicolored specks in images. This setting helps you manage the kind of noise caused by lengthy exposure times of eight seconds or more.

■ **Off.** This default setting disables long exposure noise reduction. Use it when you want the maximum amount of detail present in your photograph, even though higher noise levels will result.

■ **On.** When exposures are eight seconds or longer, the Nikon D5500 takes a second, blank exposure to compare with the first image. (While the second image is taken, the warning "Job nr" appears on the monochrome LCD monitor panel and in the viewfinder.) Noise is subtracted from your original picture, and only the noise-corrected image is saved to your memory card.

High ISO NR

Options: High, Normal (default), Low, Off

My preference: Low or Off. The D5500 does a decent job of suppressing high ISO noise, but Normal and High settings can cost you some detail. I prefer to do heavy-duty noise reduction with software, such as Adobe Photoshop or Photoshop Elements.

Noise can also be caused by higher ISO sensitivity settings. You can choose Off when you want to preserve detail at the cost of some noise graininess, and the D5500 will apply high ISO NR only at the highest ISO settings. Or, you can select High, Normal, or Low noise reduction, which is applied when ISO sensitivity has been set to ISO 800 or higher. The three variations reflect how aggressive the noise processing is (and, proportionately, how much image detail you may lose due to noise reduction).

Vignette Control

Options: High, Normal (default), Low, Off

My preference: Normal

This is the first entry in the last page of the Shooting menu. (See Figure 3.15.) Some lenses may not be up to the challenge of covering the entire frame evenly, producing darkening in the corners of your images at certain focal lengths. It's a rare defect, which is why this is the first appearance of this feature in the *D5xxx* product line.

If you consistently encounter vignetting, this option may help. It reduces darkening at the periphery of images when using lenses of the G and D type. You can choose from High, Normal, Low, and Off. It's difficult to quantify exactly how much corner-brightening each setting provides. Your best bet is to shoot some blank walls of a single color with lenses that seem to have this problem, and try a few at each of the settings. Then select the value that best seems to counter vignetting with your particular lenses.

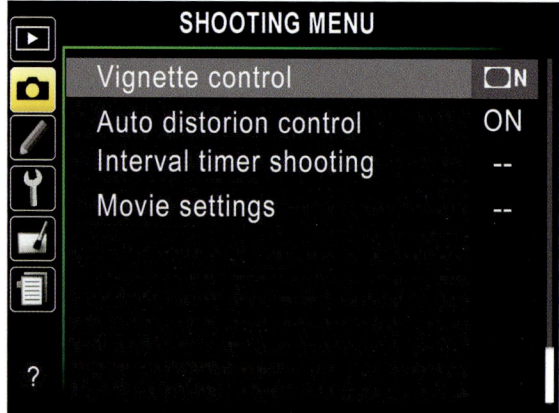

Figure 3.15
The third page of the Shooting menu.

Auto Distortion Control

Options: On, Off (default)

My preference: Off. I'd rather make these adjustments with software, such as the tools available in Photoshop and Photoshop Elements.

This option can correct barrel distortion (outward bowing of lines that should be straight) that sometimes occurs with telephoto lenses and pincushion distortion (lines that curve inward, toward the center of the frame) that can appear when using wide-angle lenses. When turned on, the D5500 uses information about your Nikon-brand lens that is stored in the (L) firmware module (and which can be updated with new firmware releases as lenses are introduced). Because this correction can result in cropping out part of your image, you may want to turn it off and use it only if you find the distortion produced by your lens is particularly bad.

Nikon recommends using this feature only with type G and D lenses (that is, lenses that have those designations as part of their names). Auto Distortion Control operates as you take the picture; you can also apply distortion control after a picture is taken using the Retouch menu (discussed in Chapter 4). Barrel and pincushion distortion can also be fully or partially corrected using an image editor like Photoshop.

Interval Timer Shooting

Options: Start, Start Options, Interval, Number of Times, Exposure Smoothing

My preference: N/A

Nikon D5500's built-in time-lapse photography feature allows you to take pictures for up to 999 intervals in bursts of as many as nine shots, with a delay of up to 23 hours and 59 minutes between shots/bursts, and an initial start-up time of as long as 23 hours and 59 minutes from the time you activate the feature. The Interval Timer Shooting screen is shown in Figure 3.16. Before you start:

1. **Set your clock.** The D5500 uses its internal World Time clock to activate, so make sure the time has been set accurately in the Setup menu before you begin.
2. **Select release mode.** If you want to shoot bursts of images each time an interval elapses, set release mode to continuous shooting. If you prefer to take one picture per interval, set the release mode dial to S. However, you can still specify multiple shots per interval when using S.

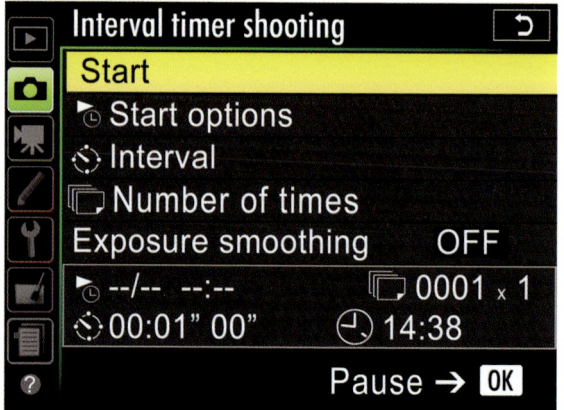

Figure 3.16
Interval Timer
Shooting options.

3. **Bracket, if desired.** If you'd like to bracket exposures during interval shooting, set up bracketing prior to beginning. (You'll learn how to bracket in Chapter 4.)

4. **Secure camera.** Mount the camera on a tripod or other secure support.

5. **Fully charge the battery.** Although the camera more or less goes to sleep between intervals, some power is drawn, and long sequences with bursts of shots can drain power even when you're not using the interval timer feature.

6. **Protect your camera.** Make sure the camera is shielded from the elements, accidents, and theft, and that the viewfinder is covered (using the DK-5 eyepiece cap if necessary) if you need to keep strong ambient light from entering the viewfinder and affecting exposure.

When you're ready to go, set up the D5500 for interval shooting:

1. **Select timer.** Choose Interval Timer Shooting from the Shooting menu.

2. **Specify a starting time.** Highlight either Now or Start Time and press the multi selector right button. If you choose Now, the interval shooting will begin approximately three seconds after you've finished setting the parameters beginning with Step 5. If you select Start Time, you'll be able to enter a specific time, as described in Steps 3 and 4.

3. **Choose start time.** When the Start Time sub-screen appears, use the multi selector left/right buttons to highlight the hours or minutes, and the up/down buttons to increase or decrease the hours/minutes entry. The 24-hour clock is used, so you can specify a time from 00:00 (midnight) to 23:59 (one minute to midnight). When both hours and minutes have been set, press the multi selector right button to move the highlighting to the Interval section of the subscreen.

4. **Set the interval between exposures.** You can use the left/right buttons to move among hours, minutes, and seconds, and use the up/down buttons to choose an interval from one second to 24 hours, but not less than the shutter speed. Press the right button when finished to move down to the number of intervals/shots per interval subscreen.

5. **Set number of intervals and shots per interval.** Use the left/right buttons to highlight the number of intervals, the number of shots taken after each interval has elapsed, and the total number of shots to be exposed overall.

6. **Start.** When all the parameters have been entered, press the multi selector right button once more, and the Start subscreen appears, with the choices On or Off. Choose either one and press OK. If you activate interval shooting, a message is displayed on the monitor one minute before each series of shots begins.

Movie Settings

Options: Frame Size/Rate, Movie Quality, Microphone, Manual Movie Settings

My preference: 1920 × 1080, 60p; High quality; Auto sensitivity

This menu entry allows you to choose four movie-making parameters. To begin shooting, rotate the Live View switch, and then push the red Movie button.

■ **Frame Size/Rate.** Choose your resolution. Use the Movie Settings entry in the Shooting menu. Or, when live view is activated, and before you start shooting your video clip, you can select the resolution/frame rate of your movie. All settings use *progressive scan,* in which all the lines are captured one after another in order. Your choices are as follows:

  ■ 1920 × 1080 at 60 fps, progressive scan (60p)

  ■ 1920 × 1080 at 30 fps, progressive scan (30p)

  ■ 1920 × 1080 at 24 fps, progressive scan (24p)

  ■ 1280 × 720 at 60 fps, progressive scan (60p)

  ■ 640 × 424 at 30 fps, progressive scan (30p)

■ **Movie Quality.** Choose High quality (to capture up to 20 minutes of action) or Normal quality (for up to 29 minutes, 59 seconds of video per clip). The High setting has a maximum bit rate requirement of 24 Mbps; if your memory card won't handle that, the Normal setting reduces the demand to 12 Mbps, at the cost of some additional compression that reduces the size of the file and cuts resolution/image quality slightly.

- **Microphone.** Here you can set audio sensitivity for the built-in stereo microphones or an optional external mic like the Nikon ME-1. Choose from Auto, High Sensitivity, Medium Sensitivity, Low Sensitivity, or Off. With the Manual Sensitivity setting, a set of volume unit (VU) meter bars appears on the menu screen showing the current sound levels. Press the right directional button to access a screen where you can select a manual sensitivity level from 1 to 20.
- **Manual Movie Settings.** Select On or Off.

Chapter 4

Custom Setting, Setup, and Retouch Menus, and My Menu

This chapter shows you how and why to use each of the options in the Custom Setting, Setup, Retouch, and My Menu sections of your D5500's menu system.

Custom Setting Menu Layout

There are 21 different Custom Settings, arranged in six different categories, as shown in Figure 4.1: Autofocus, Exposure, Timers/AE Lock, Shooting/Display, Bracketing/Flash, and Controls.

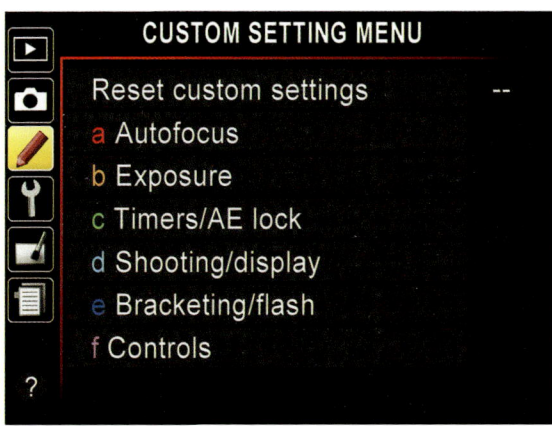

Figure 4.1
These six categories include 21 different entries in the Custom Setting menu.

For simplicity, in this book I refer to the Custom Setting menu entries by their letter/names, so that you always know that when I mention Custom Setting a4, I am describing the fourth entry in the Autofocus menu, Rangefinder. At the top level, you'll see these entries:

- Reset Custom Settings
- a. Autofocus
- b. Exposure
- c. Timers/AE Lock
- d. Shooting/Display
- e. Bracketing/Flash
- f. Controls

Reset Custom Settings

You can restore the settings of the Custom Setting banks to their default values by choosing this menu entry and selecting Yes or No.

Table 4.1 Default Custom Setting Values: Autofocus		
Function	**Option**	**Default**
a1	AF-C priority selection	Focus
a2	Number of focus points	39 points
a3	Built-in AF-assist illuminator	On
a4	Rangefinder	Off

Table 4.2 Default Custom Setting Values: Exposure		
Function	**Option**	**Default**
b1	Ev steps for exposure cntrl	1/3 step
b2	ISO display	Off

Table 4.3 Default Custom Setting Values: Timers/AE Lock		
Function	**Option**	**Default**
c1	Shutter release button AE-L	Off
c2	Auto off timers	Normal
c3	Self-timer	
	Self-timer delay	10 seconds
	Number of Shots	1
c4	Remote on duration (ML-L3)	1 minute

Table 4.4 Default Custom Setting Values: Shooting/Display

Function	Option	Default
d1	Exposure delay mode	Off
d2	File number sequence	Off
d3	Viewfinder grid display	Off
d4	Date stamp	Off
d5	Reverse indicators	-0+

Table 4.5 Default Custom Setting Values: Bracketing/Flash

Function	Option	Default
e1	Flash control for built-in flash/ Optional flash	TTL
e2	Auto bracketing set	AE

Table 4.6 Default Custom Setting Values: Controls

Function	Option	Default
f1	Assign Fn button	ISO sensitivity
f2	Assign AE-L/AF-L button	AE/AF lock
f3	Assign touch Fn	Viewfinder grid display
f4	Reverse Dial rotation	Exposure compensation/ Shutter speed/aperture

a. Autofocus

There are four red-coded Autofocus options (see Figure 4.2).

a1 AF-C Priority Selection

Options: Release, Focus (default)

My preference: Release. For the types of subjects I shoot using AF-C (sports), I want the camera to capture an image when I press the shutter, even though it may be *slightly* out of focus.

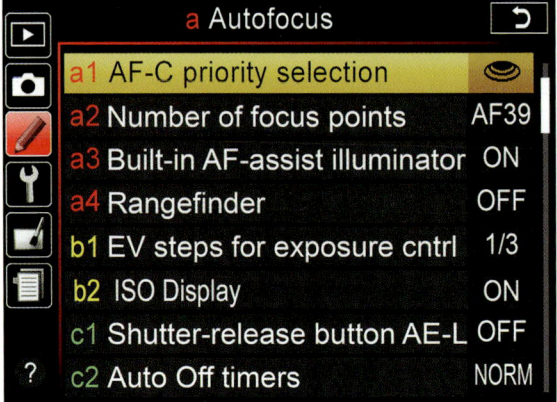

Figure 4.2
Entries in the Autofocus, Exposure, and Timers/AE lock menus.

- **Release.** When this option is selected, the shutter is activated when the release button is pushed down all the way, even if sharp focus has not yet been achieved. Because AF-C focuses and refocuses constantly when autofocus is active, you may find that an image is not quite in sharpest focus.
- **Focus.** The shutter is not activated until sharp focus is achieved with this default option. This is best for subjects that are not moving rapidly. You might miss a few shots, but you will have fewer out-of-focus images.

a2 Number of Focus Points

Options: 39 points (default), 11 points

My preference: 39 points; 11 for some sports.

You can choose the number of focus points available when you *manually* select a zone using the multi selector up/down and left/right buttons. (Note that this option is different from the 9, 21, or 39 points that may be selected *automatically* [dynamically] when using Dynamic-area AF.) Your choices are as follows:

- **39 points.** This is the default. All 39 focus points can be selected.
- **11 points.** A more widely spaced array of points is available. This can be the best choice for faster focus point selection when taking pictures of relatively large, evenly illuminated subject matter such that choosing precise focus zones is not particularly beneficial. I often use the 11-point option when photographing basketball games.

a3 Built-in AF-Assist Illuminator

Options: On (default), Off

My preference: Off. This feature isn't particularly effective and can be distracting.

Use this setting to control whether to use the AF-assist lamp built into the Nikon D5500, or rely on the more powerful AF-assist lamp built into Nikon electronic flash units (like the Nikon SB-910) and the Nikon SC-29 coiled remote flash cord (for firing the flash when not mounted on the camera).

- **On.** This default value will cause the AF-assist illuminator lamp to fire when lighting is poor, but only if single-servo autofocus (AF-S) is active, or you have selected the center focus point manually and either Single-point or Dynamic-area autofocus (rather than Auto-area autofocus) has been chosen.

- **Off.** Use this to disable the AF-assist illuminator. You'd find that useful when the lamp might be distracting or discourteous (say, at a religious ceremony or acoustic music concert), or your subject is located closer than one foot, eight inches or farther than about 10 feet.

a4 Rangefinder

Options: On, Off (default)

My preference: Off, except in dark conditions where manual focus may be tricky.

The rangefinder is a clever feature that, when activated, supplements the green focus confirmation indicator at the left edge of the viewfinder by transforming the analog exposure indicator as an "in-focus/out-of-focus" scale to show that correct focus has been achieved when focusing manually.

> **Tip**
>
> Note that this feature is not available when shooting in Manual *exposure* mode, however. The D5500 shows whether exposure is under, over, or correct, instead. Use the focus confirmation lamp to monitor manual focus in this mode.

The readout in the viewfinder is not analog (that is, continuous). Only the six indicators shown in Figure 4.3 are displayed. Two centered rectangles indicate that correct focus has been achieved; when all 12 are shown, it means that correct focus cannot be indicated. Three and six rectangles show that slight or major focus corrections are needed, respectively.

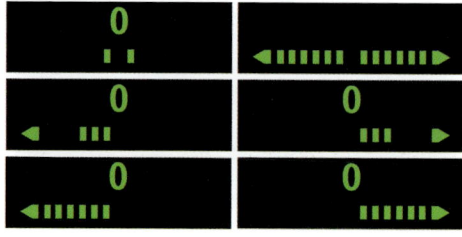

Figure 4.3

Upper left: Correct focus; upper right: focus is grossly incorrect; center left: focus slightly in front of the subject; center right: focus slightly behind the subject; bottom left: focus significantly in front of the subject; bottom right: focus significantly behind the subject.

Follow these steps to use the rangefinder:

1. Press the multi selector buttons to choose a focus point that coincides with the subject you'd like to be in focus.

2. Rotate the focusing ring, watching the rangefinder scale at the bottom of the viewfinder. If the current sharp focus plane is *in front* of the point of desired focus, the rangefinder scale will point toward the left side of the viewfinder. The greater the difference, the more bars (either three or six bars) shown in the rangefinder.

3. When the current focus plane is *behind* desired point of focus, the rangefinder indicator will point to the right.

4. When the subject you've selected with the focus zone bracket is in sharp focus, only two bars will appear, centered under the 0, and the focus confirmation indicator will stop blinking.

b. Exposure

The orange-coded Exposure setting has just two entries.

b1 EV Steps for Exposure Cntrl

Options: 1/3 step (default), 1/2 step

My preference: 1/3 step

This setting tells the Nikon D5500 the size of the "jumps" it should use when making exposure adjustments—either one-third or one-half stop. The increment you specify here applies to f/stops, shutter speeds, EV changes, and auto-exposure bracketing. As with ISO sensitivity step value, you can select from 1/3 step (the default) or 1/2 step.

Choose the 1/3 stop setting when you want the finest increments between shutter speeds and/or f/stops. For example, the D5500 will use shutter speeds such as 1/60th, 1/80th, 1/100th, 1/125th, and 1/160th second, and f/stops such as f/5.6, f/6.3, f/7.1, and f/8, giving you (and the autoexposure system) maximum flexibility.

With 1/2-stop increments, you will have larger and more noticeable changes between settings. The D5500 will apply shutter speeds such as 1/60th, 1/125th, 1/250th, and 1/500th second, and f/stops including f/5.6, f/6.7, f/8, f/9.5, and f/11. These coarser adjustments are useful when you want more dramatic changes between different exposures, or want to create a series of more widely spaced shots for high dynamic range (HDR) photography.

b2 ISO Display

Options: On, Off (default)

My preference: Off

This entry controls whether ISO or frame count are displayed in the view-finder. You have two options.

- **On.** Choose this option, and the viewfinder will display the current ISO sensitivity in the position where the frame count is normally shown. Use it if knowing the ISO setting is more important than having ready access to the number of frames remaining. (For example, you're using a very large card with thousands of exposures available.)

- **Off.** In this default mode, the number of exposures remaining is shown in the viewfinder. You can always use the information display to view the ISO setting if this mode is set.

c. Timers/AE Lock

This category is a mixed bag of settings, covering both entries that adjust delay times (c2 through c4) and how the shutter release and AE-L buttons interact (c1). (See Figure 4.4.)

c1 Shutter Release Button AE-L

Options: Off (default), On

My preference: Off

This setting allows you to separate autofocus and autoexposure activation and locking.

- **Off.** Exposure is locked *only* when the AE-L/AF-L button is pressed. This is the default.

- **On.** Exposure locks when either the shutter release button is depressed halfway or the AE-L/AF-L button is held down.

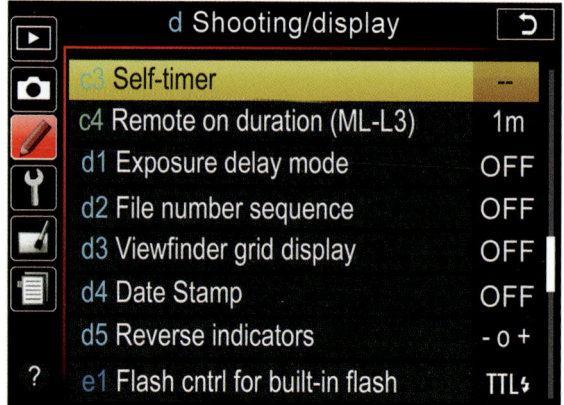

Figure 4.4
The second page of the Custom Settings menu.

c2 Auto Off Timers

Options: Short, Normal (default), Long, Custom

My preference: Normal

Use this setting to determine how long the D5500's displays and exposure meters continue to remain active after the last operation, such as autofocusing, focus point selection, and so forth, was performed. You can choose Short, Norm, or Long timings, or select Custom to specify timers for specific functions. Your options include:

- **Short.** Playback/menus: 20 seconds; Image review: 4 seconds; Live View: 5 minutes; Standby timer: 4 seconds.
- **Normal.** Playback/menus: 5 minutes; Image review: 4 seconds; Live View: 10 minutes; Standby timer: 8 seconds.
- **Long.** Playback/menus: 10 minutes; Image review: 20 seconds; Live View: 20 minutes; Standby timer: 60 seconds.
- **Custom.** Select any combination, then choose Done to confirm: Playback/menus: 8, 20, 60 seconds, 5 minutes, 10 minutes; Image review: 4, 8, 20, 60 seconds, 10 minutes; Live View: 5, 10, 15, 20, 30 minutes; Standby Timer: 4, 8, 20, 60 seconds, 30 minutes.

c3 Self-Timer

Options: Self-timer delay, Number of shots

My preference: N/A

This setting lets you choose the length of the self-timer shutter release delay, the number of shots taken, and the interval between those shots. Your options include:

- **Self-timer delay.** The default value is 10 seconds. You can also choose 2, 5, or 20 seconds. If I have the camera mounted on a tripod or other support and am too lazy to dig around for my wired or IR remote, I can set a two-second delay that is sufficient to let the camera stop vibrating after I've pressed the shutter release. I use a longer delay time if I am racing to get into the picture myself and am not sure I can make it in 10 seconds.
- **Number of shots.** After the timer finishes counting down, the D5500 can take from 1 to 9 different shots. This is a godsend when shooting photos of groups, especially if you want to appear in the photo itself. You'll always want to shoot several pictures to ensure that everyone's eyes are open and there are smiling expressions on each face. Instead of racing back and forth between the camera to trigger the self-timer multiple times, you can select the number of shots taken after a single countdown. For small groups, I always take at least as many shots as there are people in the group—plus one. That gives everybody a chance to close their eyes. Of course, the ML-L3 IR remote is often your best choice, but this facility works well if you don't have one handy.

c4 Remote on Duration (ML-L3)

Options: 1 minute (default), 5, 10, 15 minutes

My preference: N/A

You can adjust the amount of time the D5500 "looks" for an IR signal from its front and rear infrared sensors when using the ML-L3 IR remote. You can select 1, 5, 10, or 15 minutes. Use a shorter active interval to save power. This setting has no effect on the Nikon WR-10 remote system.

d. Shooting/Display

This menu section (see Figure 4.4, shown earlier) offers a variety of mostly unrelated shooting and display options not found elsewhere, but which are not frequently changed, making them suitable for a Custom Setting entry.

d1 Exposure Delay Mode

Options: On, Off (default)

My preference: Off

This is a marginally useful feature you can use to force the Nikon D5500 to snap a picture about one second after you've pressed the shutter release button all the way. It's useful when you are using shutter speeds of about 1/8th to 1/60th second hand-held and want to minimize the effects of the vibration that results when you depress the shutter button. It can also be used when the camera is mounted on a tripod, although the self-timer function, set to a two-second delay, is more useful in that scenario. When switched On, the camera will pause while you steady your steely grip on the camera, taking the picture about one second later. When turned Off, the picture is taken when the shutter release is pressed, as normal.

d2 File Number Sequence

Options: On, Off (default), Reset

My preference: Off

The Nikon D5500 will automatically apply a file number to each picture you take, using consecutive numbering for all your photos over a long period of time, spanning many different memory cards, starting over from scratch when you insert a new card, or when you manually reset the numbers. Numbers are applied from 0001 to 9999, at which time the D5500 "rolls over" to 0001 again.

The camera keeps track of the last number used in its internal memory and, if File Number Sequence is turned On, will apply a number that's one higher, or a number that's one higher than the largest number in the current folder on the memory card inserted in the camera. You can also start over each time a new folder has been created on the memory card, or reset the current counter back to 0001 at any time.

Here's how it works:

- **On.** At this setting, the D5500 will use the number stored in its internal memory any time a new folder is created, a new memory card is inserted, or an existing memory card is formatted. If the card is not blank and contains images, then the next number will be one greater than the highest number on the card *or* in internal memory (whichever is higher).

- **Off.** If you're using a blank/reformatted memory card, or a new folder is created, the next photo taken will be numbered 0001. File number sequences will be reset every time you use or format a card, or a new folder is created (which happens when an existing folder on the card contains 999 shots).

- **Reset.** The D5500 assigns a file number that's one larger than the largest file number in the current folder, unless the folder is empty, in which case numbering is reset to 0001. At this setting, new or reformatted memory cards will always have 0001 as the first file number.

d3 Viewfinder Grid Display

Options: On, Off (default)

My preference: Off

Activates the optional grid guidelines in the viewfinder, which are useful for aligning the horizon, vertical lines, and especially for framing architectural subjects.

d4 Date Stamp

Options: Off (default), Date, Date/Time, Date Counter

My preference: N/A

You can superimpose the date, time, or both on your photographs, or imprint a date counter that shows the number of days (or years and days, or months, years, and days) between when the picture was taken and a date (in the past or future) that you select. The good news is that this feature can be useful for certain types of photographs used for documentation. The bad news, especially if you use the feature accidentally, is that the imprint is a permanent part of the photograph. You'll have to polish up your Photoshop skills if you want to remove it, or, at the very least, crop it out of the picture area. Date and time are set using the format you specify in the Time and Date setting of the Setup menu.

Your options are as follows:

- **Off.** Deactivates the date/time imprint feature.
- **Date.** The date is overlaid on your image in the bottom-right corner of the frame, and appears in the shooting information display. If you've turned on Auto Image Rotation the date is overlaid at the bottom-right corner of vertically oriented frames.
- **Date/Time.** Both date and time are imprinted, in the same positions.
- **Date Counter.** This option imprints the current date on the image, but also adds the number of days that have elapsed since a particular date in the past that you specify, *or* the days remaining until an upcoming date in the future.

d5 Reverse Indicators

Options: -0+ (default), +0-

My preference: -0+

You can use the options in this menu entry to change the behavior of the command dials. Use the available tweaks to change the behavior of the dials to better suit your preferences, or if you're coming to the Nikon world from another vendor's product that uses a different operational scheme. Keep in mind that redefining basic controls in this way can prove confusing if someone other than yourself uses your camera, or if you find yourself working with other Nikon cameras that have retained the normal command dial behavior. The reason that the dials are set for their default directions is to match the direction of rotation of the aperture ring/command dial (when changing the aperture). Turning any of the three to the left decreases exposure, while rotating to the right increases exposure.

e. Bracketing/Flash

There are just two settings in this submenu that deal with bracketing and electronic flash (hence the cleverly concocted name). I'll provide a complete rundown of flash options in Chapter 5. Here, I'll offer an introduction to the settings at your disposal.

e1 Flash Cntrl for Built-in Flash

Options: TTL/Optional Flash, Manual

My preference: N/A

The Nikon D5500's built-in flash has two modes, which I'll describe in a lot more detail in Chapter 5. Your options are as follows (the options change when a Nikon SB-400 or SB-500 external flash is attached and powered up, so you can adjust that unit instead):

- **TTL.** When the built-in flash is triggered, the D5500 first fires a pre-flash and measures the light reflected back and through the lens to calculate the proper exposure when the full flash is emitted a fraction of a second later. When the SB-400 or SB-500 flash are mounted, this entry changes to Optional flash. With the SB-500, you can set the Commander mode for the attached flash unit.

- **Manual.** You can set the level of the built-in flash from full power to a fraction that will depend on which flash you are using, ranging from 1/32 to 1/64 or 1/128 power.

e2 Auto Bracketing Set

Options: AE (default), WB, ADL

My preference: AE

The Nikon D5500 can automatically take several pictures using slightly different settings within a range that you specify, and apply the changes to automatic exposure, electronic flash, or white balance. This setting allows you to specify whether bracketing is used for automatic exposure only (AE), white balance color bracketing alone (WB bracketing), or Active D-Lighting bracketing. No autoexposure or flash bracketing will be performed when white balance bracketing is activated. Because you can specify white balance manually when importing a RAW file, WB bracketing is not available when Quality has been set to NEF (RAW) or NEF (RAW)+JPEG. The results you get with flash bracketing can vary quite a bit, depending on the amount of ambient illumination and flash mode you've chosen, but exposure bracketing is fairly consistent. I tend to leave this option set to AE most of the time. White balance bracketing is useful when you're not quite sure of the color balance of your illumination.

f. Controls

You can modify the way various control buttons and dials perform by using the options in this submenu, shown in Figure 4.5.

f1 Assign Fn. Button

Options: Quality, ISO sensitivity (default), White Balance, Active D-Lighting, HDR, +NEF (RAW), BKT, AF-area mode, Viewfinder grid display, Wi-Fi

My preference: N/A

You can define the function of the Fn button. Your choices are as follows:

- **Quality.** When this behavior is selected, pressing the Fn button produces the information edit screen, with Quality/Size options highlighted. You can rotate the command dial to cycle among all the combinations of image quality and size (resolution). Release the Fn button to lock the combination you've dialed in.

- **ISO sensitivity.** Choose this option, the default, and pressing the Fn button produces the information edit screen, with ISO sensitivity settings highlighted. You can rotate the command dial to change values. Release the Fn button to lock the setting.

- **White balance.** When this behavior is selected, pressing the Fn button produces the information edit screen, with white balance highlighted. You can rotate the command dial to change the WB setting. Release the Fn button to lock the WB setting you've dialed in.

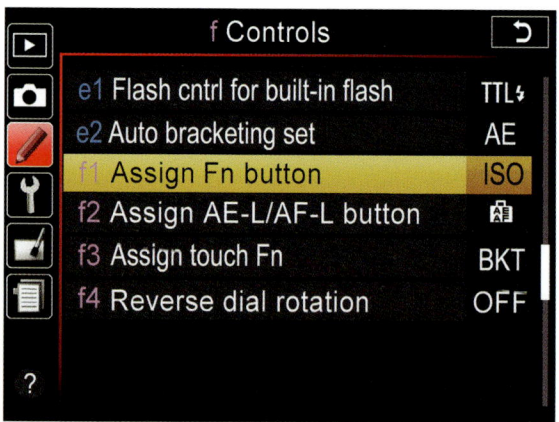

Figure 4.5

Controls submenu.

- **Active D-Lighting.** Press the Fn button and rotate the command dial to choose Active D-Lighting settings.
- **HDR.** Allows using the Fn button to turn HDR functions on or off when using P, S, A, or M modes. HDR is deactivated after you've taken a picture, or when you press the Fn button a second time.
- **+NEF (RAW).** If your D5500 is currently set to shoot JPEG only, use this setting so that when you press the Fn button, the next shot will be recorded as a RAW+JPEG set. I use this option when shooting sports or other fast-moving events, then decide to shoot an image, say, along the sidelines, that could benefit from RAW manipulation later.
- **BKT.** Press the Fn button when using P, S, A, or M modes and rotate the control dial to choose a bracketing increment for exposure or white balance bracketing, or to turn ADL bracketing on or off.
- **AF-area mode.** Press the Fn button when using P, S, A, or M modes and rotate the control dial to choose any of the AF-area modes described in Chapter 5, including Single-point, Dynamic-area (9 points), Dynamic-area (21 points), Dynamic-area (39 points), or 3D-tracking.
- **Viewfinder Grid display.** The Fn button allows you to turn viewfinder grid display on or off.
- **Wi-Fi.** The Fn button can be used to access Wi-Fi options.

f2 Assign AE-L/AF-L Button

Options: AE/AF Lock (default), AE Lock Only, AF Lock Only, AE Lock (Hold), AF-ON

My preference: AF-ON for back button focus

As if the Nikon D5500 didn't have enough buttons that are user-definable, you can change the behavior of the AE-L/AF-L button, too! The default value for the AE-L/AF-L button is AE/AF Lock. To recap your options:

- **AE/AF Lock.** Lock both focus and exposure while the AE-L/AF-L button is pressed.
- **AE Lock Only.** Lock only the exposure while the AE-L/AF-L button is pressed.
- **AF Lock Only.** Focus is locked in while the AE-L/AF-L button is held down.
- **AE Lock (Hold).** Exposure is locked when the AE-L/AF-L button is pressed, and remains locked until the button is pressed again, or the exposure meter–off delay expires.
- **AF-ON.** The AE-L/AF-L button is used to initiate autofocus.

f3 Assign Touch Fn

Options: Focus-point selection, ISO sensitivity, Active D-Lighting, HDR, BRK, AF-area Mode, Viewfinder grid display (default), Aperture

My preference: Disable

This is sort of a weird option, which allows you to set certain controls by sliding a finger across the touch screen. To use it, just follow these steps:

1. **Enable.** Make sure Touch Controls are activated, Info Display Auto Off is set to On, and Auto Off Timers are set to Short, or, if you have custom timings (as detailed earlier in this chapter), Playback/Menus and Standby Timers are set for a short period of time. That's because Touch Functions works *only* when the LCD display turns off.

2. **Define a behavior.** Select one of the behaviors listed below.

3. **Activate behavior.** When the monitor turns off automatically (you can force it to turn off by pressing the Info button, too), slide your finger on the Touch Function area to make the adjustment.

4. **Use Touch Function area only.** When the LCD monitor is in the normal position against the camera body, the Touch Function area consists of the right half of the screen. When the LCD monitor is extended (*but not facing forward toward your subject*), the Touch Function area consists of the entire screen. Extended is often the best configuration when using Touch Fn, because your face will not touch the monitor as you work. This limitation is the chief reason why I don't use this feature very much.

You can activate one of the following behaviors for the Touch Function:

- **Focus-point selection.** If you've chosen a focus point selection mode *other* than Auto-area AF (which means the D5500 always selects the focus area for you), you can slide a finger over the Touch Fn area to specify the focus point. You'll be able to track the movement of the focus point in the viewfinder.

- **ISO sensitivity.** Choose this option and slide a finger across the Touch Fn area to change the ISO value.

- **Active D-Lighting.** Slide a finger over the Touch Fn area to choose Active D-Lighting settings when using P, S, A, or M exposure modes.

- **HDR.** Slide a finger over the Touch Fn area to adjust HDR functions on or off when using P, S, A, or M modes.

- **BKT.** Slide a finger over the Touch Fn area when using P, S, A, or M exposure modes to choose a bracketing increment or to turn ADL bracketing on or off.

- **AF-area mode.** Slide a finger over the Touch Fn area to choose an AF-area mode.
- **Viewfinder grid display.** The Touch Fn area allows you to turn viewfinder grid display on or off.
- **Aperture.** Slide a finger over the Touch Fn area to adjust aperture in Aperture-priority and Manual exposure modes.

f4 Reverse Dial Rotation

Options: Exposure compensation, Shutter speed/aperture

My preference: N/A

You can reverse the rotation direction of the command dial separately for exposure compensation and shutter speed/aperture setting using the check boxes that appear when this menu entry is selected.

Setup Menu Options

There is a long list of entries in the orange-coded Setup menu, identified by a wrench symbol (see Figure 4.6), in which you can make additional adjustments on how your camera *behaves* before or during your shooting session, as differentiated from the Shooting menu, which adjusts how the pictures are actually taken. Your choices include:

- Format Memory Card
- Image Comment
- Copyright Information
- Time Zone and Date
- Language
- Beep Options
- Touch Controls
- Monitor Brightness
- Info Display Format
- Auto Info Display
- Info Display Auto Off
- Clean Image Sensor
- Lock Mirror Up for Cleaning
- Image Dust Off Ref Photo
- Flicker Reduction
- Slot Empty Release Lock
- Video Mode
- HDMI
- Accessory Terminal
- Wi-Fi
- Eye-Fi Upload
- Conformity Marking
- Firmware Version

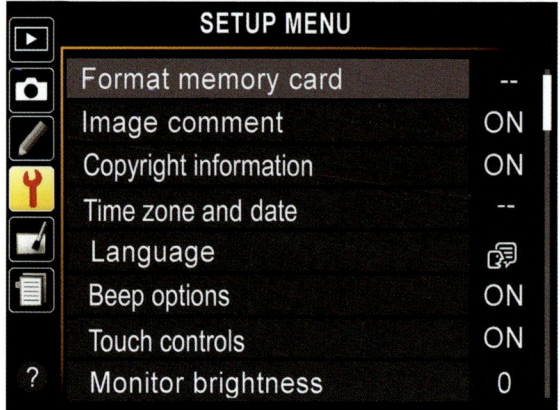

Figure 4.6
The Setup menu allows you to adjust how the D5500 behaves.

Format Memory Card

Options: Yes, No

My preference: N/A

I recommend using this menu entry to reformat your memory card after each shoot to avoid stray files and to set up a fresh file system. To format a memory card, choose this entry from the Setup menu, highlight Yes on the screen that appears, and press OK.

Image Comment

Options: Enter comment

My preference: N/A

The image comment is your opportunity to add a copyright notice, personal information about yourself (including contact info), or even a description of where the image was taken (e.g., Browns Super Bowl 2016), although text entry with the Nikon D5500 is a bit too clumsy for doing a lot of individual annotation of your photos. (But you still might want to change the comment each time, say, you change cities during your travels.) The embedded comments can be read by many software programs, including Nikon ViewNX or Capture NX.

The standard text entry screen described earlier in Chapter 3 can be used to enter your comment, with up to 36 characters available. For the copyright symbol, embed a lowercase "c" within opening and closing parentheses: (c). You can input the comment, turn attachment of the comment On or Off using the Attach Comment entry, and select Done when you're finished working with comments. If you find typing with a cursor too tedious, you can enter your comment in Nikon Capture NX and upload it to the camera through a USB cable.

Copyright Information

Options: Enter copyright information

My preference: N/A

This is an expansion of the Image Comment capability, allowing you to specify the name of the "artist" (photographer), and enter copyright information. Use the standard Nikon text entry screen described earlier. Highlight the Attach Copyright Information option and press the right multi selector button to mark/unmark it to control whether your copyright data is embedded in each photo as taken.

Time Zone and Date

Options: Time zone, Date and time, Date format, Daylight saving time

My preference: N/A

Use this menu entry to adjust the D5500's internal clock. Your options include:

- **Time zone.** A small map will pop up on the setting screen and you can choose your local time zone. I sometimes forget to change the time zone when I travel (especially when going to Europe), so my pictures are all time-stamped incorrectly. I like to use the time stamp to recall exactly when a photo was taken, so keeping this setting correct is important.
- **Date and time.** Use this setting to enter the exact year, month, day, hour, minute, and second, using a 24-hour clock.
- **Date format.** Choose from Y/M/D (year/month/day), M/D/Y (month/day/year), or D/M/Y (day/month/year) formats.
- **Daylight saving time.** Use this to turn daylight saving time On or Off. Because the date on which DST goes into effect each year has been changed from time to time, if you turn this feature on you may need to monitor your camera to make sure DST has been implemented correctly.

Language

Options: Languages

My preference: Inglés

Choose your language for menu display, including Arabic, Chinese (Simplified and Traditional), Czech, Danish, Dutch, English, Finnish, French, German, Greek, Hindi, Hungarian, Indonesian, Italian, Japanese, Korean, Norwegian, Polish, Portuguese (Portugal and Brazil), Romanian, Russian, Spanish, Swedish, Thai, Turkish, and Ukrainian.

Beep Options

Options: Beep On, Off, Off (Touch Controls); Pitch (default Low)

My preference: Off

The Nikon D5500's internal beeper provides a (usually) superfluous chirp to signify various functions, such as the countdown of your camera's self-timer or autofocus confirmation in AF-S mode. You can (and probably should) switch it off if you want to avoid the beep because it's annoying, impolite, distracting (at a concert or museum), or undesired for any other reason. Select from:

- **Beep On/Off.** Your options include On, Off, and Off (touch controls only).
- **Pitch.** Select High or Low pitches for your sounds.

Touch Controls

Options: Enable (default), Playback Only, Disable

My preference: Enable

You can go with the default choice, Enable, to leave the touch controls active at all times. If you find yourself using the touch controls during shooting by accident, you can select Playback Only to retain the ability to select and scroll among images by touch, or disable touch controls entirely. You must have touch controls enabled to use the Touch Function feature described earlier.

Monitor Brightness

Options: –5 to +5 (default 0)

My preference: N/A

Choose this menu option and a grayscale strip appears on the LCD, as shown in Figure 4.7. Use the controls to adjust the brightness to a comfortable viewing level. Under the lighting conditions that exist when you make this adjustment, you should be able to see all 10 swatches from black to white. If the two end swatches blend together, the brightness has been set too low. If the two whitest swatches on the right end of the strip blend together, the brightness is too high. Brighter settings use more battery power, but can allow you to view an image on the LCD outdoors in bright sunlight. When you have the brightness you want, press/tap OK to lock it in and return to the menu.

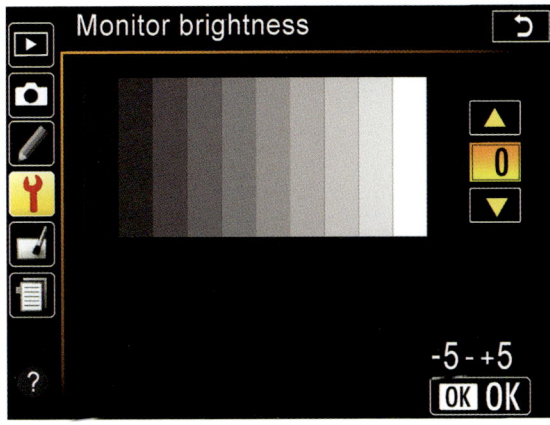

Figure 4.7
Adjust LCD monitor brightness.

Info Display Format

Options: Six options each for Auto, Scene, Special Effects, or PSAM modes; Default: Graphic

My preference: I don't use Graphic display for any exposure mode.

This entry, the first in the second page of the Setup menu (see Figure 4.8), allows you to choose the shooting information screen format and color scheme. You can select the Classic format, which I find easier to read and use, with background colors of blue, black, or white, or the Graphic format with background colors of green, black, or brown. Helpful thumbnails of each display format are shown as a preview of what your screens will look like. You can

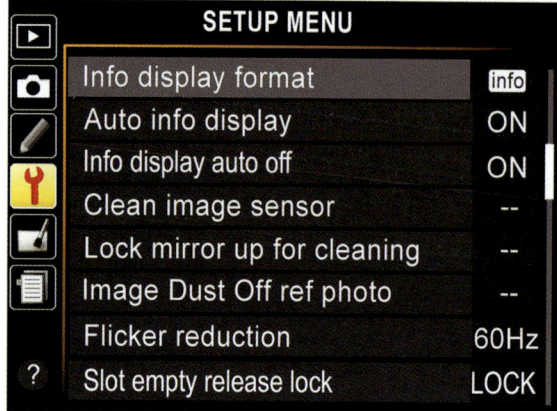

Figure 4.8
The second page of the Setup menu.

select separate looks for Auto/Scene/Special Effects modes and Program/ Shutter-priority/Aperture-priority/Manual modes.

Your selection is strictly a matter of personal preference. You can, for example, use Classic format for the semi-automatic/manual modes that you'll probably be working with most of the time, and opt for Graphic format for the automatic modes that may be preferred by a less photo-savvy family member or friend who also works with your D5500 from time to time.

Auto Info Display

Options: On (default), Off

My preference: On

Choose On, and the shooting information display will appear automatically after the shutter release is pressed halfway, and after the picture is taken if image review has been turned off in the Playback menu. Choose Off, and the information display can be viewed by pressing the information edit button. Some find that Off is less distracting, because the information display is only shown when invoked by the user.

Info Display Auto Off

Options: On (default), Off

My preference: On

Choose On, and the shooting information display will disappear automatically after the period specified in the Custom Setting c2, Auto Off Timers, option (either Short, Normal, or Long, or your custom setting for Standby Timer). You can select the period you like, but you should remember that the Touch Function feature works only after the display has disappeared from the screen.

Clean Image Sensor

Options: Clean Now, Clean At (ON, OFF, ON/OFF, Cleaning Off)

My preference: N/A

This entry gives you some control over the Nikon D5500's automatic sensor cleaning feature. Select from:

- **ON.** Clean at startup.
- **OFF.** Clean at shutdown.
- **ON/OFF.** Clean at both startup and shutdown.
- **Cleaning Off.** No automatic dust removal will be performed. Use this to preserve battery power, or if you prefer to use automatic dust removal only when you explicitly want to apply it.

Lock Mirror Up for Cleaning

Options: Lock mirror up

My preference: N/A

You can also clean the sensor manually. Use this menu entry to raise the mirror and open the shutter so you'll have access to the sensor for cleaning with a blower, brush, or swab. This option is available only when sufficient battery power (at least 60 percent) is available. Use a fully charged battery or connect the D5500 to an EP-5a/EH5b AC adapter.

Image Dust Off Ref Photo

Options: Start; Clean Sensor, then Start

My preference: N/A

This menu choice lets you "take a picture" of any dust or other particles that may be adhering to your sensor. The D5500 will then append information about the location of this dust to your photos, so that the Image Dust Off option in Capture NX can be used to mask the dust in the NEF image.

To use this feature, select Image Dust Off Ref Photo, choose either Start, or Clean Sensor and then Start, and then press OK. If directed to do so, the camera will first perform a self-cleaning operation by applying ultrasonic vibration to the low-pass filter that resides on top of the sensor. Then, a screen will appear asking you to take a photo of a bright featureless white object 10cm from the lens. Nikon recommends using a lens with a focal length of at least 50mm. Point the D5500 at a solid-white card and press the shutter release. An image with the extension NDF will be created, and can be used by Nikon Capture NX as a reference photo if the "dust off" picture is placed in the same folder as an image to be processed for dust removal.

Flicker Reduction

Options: Auto (default), 50Hz, 60Hz

My preference: N/A

This option reduces flicker and banding, which can occur when shooting in Live View mode and Movie mode under fluorescent and mercury vapor illumination, because the cycling of these light sources interacts with the frame rate of the camera's video system. In the United States, you'd choose the 60Hz frequency; in locations where 50Hz current is the norm, select that option instead. You can also select Auto and let the camera decide.

Slot Empty Release Lock

Options: Release Locked (default), Enable Release

My preference: Release Locked

This option gives you the ability to snap off "pictures" without a memory card installed—or to lock the camera shutter release if that is the case. It is sometimes called play mode, because you can experiment with your camera's features or even hand your D5500 to a friend to let them fool around, without any danger of pictures actually being taken.

Video Mode

Options: NTSC, PAL

My preference: NTSC (Never Twice the Same Color)

This setting, the first on the third page of the Setup menu (see Figure 4.9), controls the output of the Nikon D5500 to a conventional video system through the video cable when you're displaying images on a monitor or connected to a VCR through the external device's yellow video input jack. You can select NTSC, used in the United States, Canada, Mexico, many Central and South American, and Caribbean countries, much of Asia, and other countries, or PAL, which is used in the UK, much of Europe, Africa, India, China, and parts of the Middle East.

HDMI

Options: Output Resolution: Auto (default), 1080p, 1080i, 720p, 576p, 480p; Device Control: On (default), Off

My preference: Auto

The Nikon D5500 has a High-Definition Multimedia Interface (HDMI) video connection, so you can play back your camera's images on HDTV or HD monitors using a type C cable, such as the Nikon HC-E1 cable, which Nikon does not provide to you, but which is readily available from third parties. Before you link up you'll want to choose the HDMI resolution to be used, from 480p (640 × 480 progressive scan); 576p (720 × 576 progressive scan); 720p (1280 × 720 progressive scan); or 1080i (1920 × 1080 interlaced scan). Or, select the Auto option and the camera will choose the appropriate format for you.

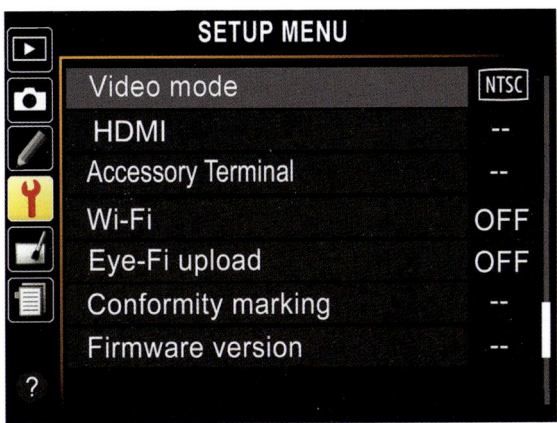

Figure 4.9
Video Mode is the first entry in the third page of the Setup menu.

You can also choose to turn Device Control on or off. When On is chosen and the camera is connected to a television that supports the HDMI-CEC protocol (when both the TV and camera are turned on), you'll see PLAY and SLIDE SHOW messages on the television. You can then use the television's compatible remote control instead of the multi selector and OK buttons to review images and play slide shows. Choose Off, and this capability is disabled.

Accessory Terminal

Options: Remote Control: Remote Shutter Release (Take Photos, Record Movies); Assign Fn Button: Same as Camera AE-L/AF-L button, Live View; Location Data: Standby Timer (On, Off), Position, Set Clock from Satellite (On, Off)

My preference: N/A

This setting has two distinct functions, Remote Control, which determines the behavior of the Nikon D5500 when using a wired remote cord such as the Nikon MC-DC2, or wireless remote controller like the ML-L3 infrared remote. You can choose whether to take still photographs or start movie capture. It also is used to work with Location Data if you've connected an optional Nikon GP-1a GPS device to your camera.

Your options for the Remote Control submenu are as follows:

- **Remote Shutter Release.** Select either of these two behaviors for the shutter release button on your remote control:
  - **Take photos.** Press the shutter release button on the wired or wireless remote to take a still photograph. The response of the camera will depend on the release mode you've selected, from among the single shot, continuous, quiet mode, self-timer, and delayed/quick response ML-L3 options described earlier.
  - **Record movies.** Press the shutter release button on the wired or wireless remote halfway to initiate live view (it's not necessary to use the Lv switch on top of the camera), or to start autofocus (either AF-S or AF-F, as you selected) if live view is already active. Then, press down all the way to start or end movie capture. When you stop recording, live view will continue. It must be deactivated using the Lv switch on the camera.

■ **Assign Fn Button.** You can select either of these two options:

   ■ **Same as camera AE-L/AF-L button.** The Fn button on the wireless remote control performs the same function you've currently defined to the camera's AE-L/AF-L button, using Custom Setting f2, as described earlier.

   ■ **Live view.** The Fn button on the remote control starts/ends live view. I use this when I have the camera set up on a tripod, and want to use the wireless remote to start or stop live view (thus reducing the amount of time live view is active and draining my battery), while using the same remote's shutter release button to take a photo or record movies.

The Location Data submenu produces a different set of adjustments. This menu entry has options for using the Nikon GP-1/GP1a Global Positioning System (GPS) device. It has three options, none of which turn GPS features on or off, despite the misleading "Enable" and "Disable" nomenclature (what you're enabling and disabling is the automatic exposure meter turn-off):

■ **Standby Timer.** Setting to Enable reduces battery drain by enabling turning off exposure meters while using the GP-1/1a after the time specified in Custom Setting c2, Standby Timer, has elapsed. When the meters turn off, the GP-1/1a becomes inactive and must reacquire at least three satellite signals before it can begin recording GPS data once more. Setting to Disable causes exposure meters to remain on while using the GP-1/1a, so that GPS data can be recorded at any time, despite increased battery drain.

■ **Position.** This is an information display, rather than a selectable option. It appears when the GP-1/1a is connected and receiving satellite positioning data. It shows the latitude, longitude, altitude, and Coordinated Universal Time (UTC) values.

■ **Set Clock from Satellite.** Choose Yes to allow the camera to update its internal clock from information provided by the GPS device when attached. No disables this updating feature. You might want to avoid updating the clock if you're traveling and want all the basic date/time information embedded in your image files to reflect the settings back home, rather than the date and time where your pictures are taken. Note that if the GPS device is active when shooting, the local date and time will be embedded in the GPS portion of the EXIF data.

Wi-Fi

Options: Network Connection, Network Settings

My preference: N/A

This entry is used to set up the D5500's built-in Wi-Fi system to link to your smart phone, tablet, or phablet, (using either iOS or Android operating systems). All these capabilities are very cool. Wi-Fi uploads can provide instant backup of important shots and sharing, as well as camera control.

Connecting Your Camera to Your Smart Device

To use your D5500's built-in Wi-Fi capabilities, you must first install Nikon's Wireless Mobile Device app on your smart device. Visit the Google Play service, Apple's App Store, or another app marketplace and download the free Nikon wireless mobile utility. Then:

1. **Activate Wi-Fi.** In the Wi-Fi entry of the Setup menu, choose Network Connection, select Enable, and press the OK button. A "Waiting for Connection" prompt appears on the Wi-Fi screen of the D5500.

2. **Activate your smart device connection.** Go to your device's Settings screen and choose the adapter's Wi-Fi network SSID as the device's current Wi-Fi connection. The name will be something on the order of Nikon_WU_*nnnnnnnn*. (This step will be different for each particular device.) Unfortunately, there are many different ways to connect the D5500 to your smart device, and it's not possible to cover all of them. Depending on what device you own, you may have a feature called Push-Button WPS, PIN-entry WPS, or a View SSID linkup. Apple's iOS is generally simpler, using the View SSID option. On my iPhone 5s, there's a "Wi-Fi" entry between the Airplane Mode and Bluetooth entries in the main Settings screen. I just selected the camera's ID and I was connected.

3. **Open the Wireless Mobile Adapter app.** You should be connected, and the Take Photos and View Photos menu will be visible (see Figure 4.10, left). If you want to check your connection, battery level, and adapter firmware version, you can tap the gear icon in the upper-right corner of the app.

4. **Shift your phone/tablet to live view.** Tap the Take Photos entry and you'll hear the mirror of your D5500 flip up as the camera switches to live view and transmits the sensor image to your device. (See Figure 4.10, center.)

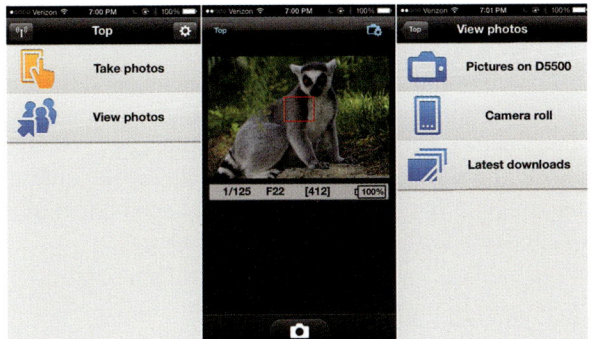

Figure 4.10
Activate Take Photo or View Photo options (left); see your camera's live view and capture images (center); or view photos on the camera or your smart device (right).

5. **Evaluate preview image.** The live view preview will show up on your device's screen (unless you choose to turn it off), with shooting data such as current f/stop, shutter speed, and remaining exposures displayed.

6. **Set focus.** A red focus frame is shown in the fame. You can tap anywhere in the frame to move the focus frame to another part of the image. The red frame turns green when the subject is in focus.

7. **Take photo.** Tap the camera icon in the lower part of the screen to take a picture.

8. **Download file to smart device (automatically).** The image you just took will automatically download to your device (unless you disable this feature) and become available for review in a strip at the bottom of the phone/tablet's live view screen.

9. **Download files to smart device (manually).** If automatic download is not enabled, images will remain on the D5500's memory card until you explicitly download them during playback on the camera. As you review images on the D5500's LCD, you can select Playback options by pressing the information edit (*i*) button. Choose Select to Send to Smart Device/ Deselect, and mark the images you want to upload. Press OK to commence the upload to a connected smart device.

10. **View photos.** You can evaluate the photos downloaded to your smart device by tapping the View Photos option on the main screen. The iOS version is shown in Figure 4.10 (right), with options to view still images on the camera's memory card, the device's Camera Roll, or recent downloads. (Movies cannot be viewed or downloaded.)

The app has a number of options, such as the ability to turn device live view on or off (you'll no longer see a real-time view of what the camera sees). You can also activate the self-timer (so you can get in the picture yourself without needing to have the phone/tablet in your hand) and activate/deactivate automatic downloading of the camera's shots to your device. Pictures that you take that are downloaded to your phone/tablet are also stored on the D5500's memory card, so you can use the app to *take* pictures (like a remote control) even if you don't want to download/store them on your phone or tablet.

Eye-Fi Upload

Options: Enable (default), Disable

My preference: Disable

This option is displayed in the menu *only* when a compatible Eye-Fi memory card is being used in the D5500. The Eye-Fi card looks like an ordinary SDHC memory card, but has built-in Wi-Fi capabilities, so it can be used to transmit your photos as they are taken directly to a computer over a Wi-Fi network. An advantage of Eye-Fi cards is that they can uploaded directly to Facebook and many other social venues.

Conformity Marking

Options: None

My preference: N/A

Digital cameras, like other devices, must meet various product standards, which can change from time to time, and may even vary from country to country. You can see some of these "seals of approval" on the bottom of your Nikon D5500. This menu entry allows Nikon to modify the camera's conformity notices through firmware updates. It has no real function or purpose for end users.

Firmware Version

Options: View version, Update

My preference: N/A

You can see the current firmware release in use in the menu listing.

Retouch Menu

In the Retouch menu you'll find a handful of adjustments and special effects you can apply in the camera to photographs you've already taken.

- NEF (Raw Processing)
- Trim
- Resize
- D-Lighting
- Quick Retouch
- Red-Eye Correction
- Straighten
- Distortion Control
- Perspective Control
- Fisheye
- Filter Effects

- Monochrome
- Image Overlay
- Color Outline
- Photo Illustration
- Color Sketch
- Miniature Effect
- Selective Color
- Painting
- Edit Movie
- Side-by-Side Comparison

The Retouch menu (see Figure 4.11) is most useful when you want to create a modified copy of an image on the spot, for immediate printing or e-mailing without first importing into your computer for more extensive editing. You can also use it to create a JPEG version of an image in the camera when you are shooting RAW-only photos. While you can retouch images that have already been processed by the Retouch menu, each retouch option can be applied only once, except for the Image Overlay and Edit Movie tools. You may notice some quality loss when applying more than one retouch option.

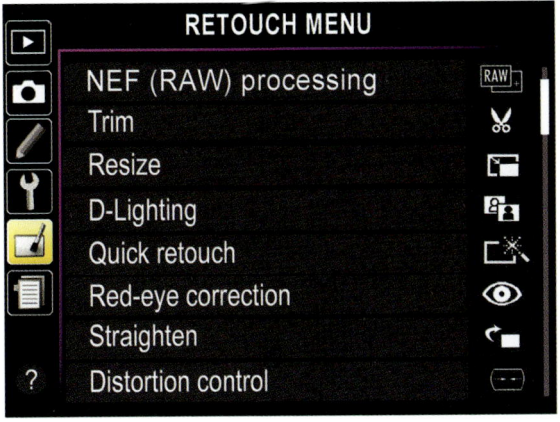

Figure 4.11
The Retouch menu allows simple in-camera editing.

To create a retouched copy of an image:

1. While browsing among images in Playback mode, press the *i* button when an image you want to retouch is displayed on the screen. Highlight Retouch and press the OK button. Then, the Retouch menu will pop up, and you can select a retouching option.

2. From the Retouch menu, select the option you want and press the multi selector right button. The Nikon D5500's standard image selection screen appears. Scroll among the images as usual with the left/right multi selector buttons, press the Zoom In button to examine a highlighted image more closely, and press OK to choose that image.

3. Work with the options available from that particular Retouch menu feature and press OK to create the modified copy, or Playback to cancel your changes.

4. A retouched JPEG image will be the same size and quality as the original, except for copies created from NEF images (which are always saved as JPEG Fine images).

NEF (RAW) Processing

Options: User settings

My preference: N/A

Use this tool to create a JPEG version of any image saved in either straight RAW (with no JPEG version) or RAW+Basic (with a Basic JPEG version). You can select from among several parameters to "process" your new JPEG copy right in the camera.

1. Choose a RAW image. Select NEF (RAW) processing from the Retouch menu. You'll be shown the standard Nikon D5500 image selection screen. Use the left/right buttons or touch screen to navigate among the RAW images displayed. Tap or press OK to select the highlighted image.

2. In the NEF (RAW) processing screen, you can use the multi selector up/down keys to select from nine different attributes of the RAW image information to apply to your JPEG copy. Choose Image Quality (Fine, Normal, or Basic), Image Size (Large, Medium, or Small), White Balance, Exposure Compensation, Picture Control, High ISO Noise Reduction, Color Space, and D-Lighting parameters.

Tip

The White Balance parameter cannot be selected for images created with the Image Overlay tool, and the Preset manual white balance setting can be fine-tuned only with images that were originally shot using the Preset white balance setting. Exposure compensation cannot be adjusted for images taken using Active D-Lighting, and both white balance and optimize image settings cannot be applied to pictures taken using any of the Scene modes.

3. Press the Zoom In button to magnify the image temporarily while the button is held down, or use the touch controls.

4. Press or tap Playback if you change your mind, to exit from the processing screen.

5. When all parameters are set, highlight EXE (for Execute) and press OK. The D5500 will create a JPEG file with the settings you've specified, and show an Image Saved message on the LCD when finished.

Trim

Options: 3:2, 4:3, 5:4, 1:1, 16:9 aspect ratios

My preference: N/A

This option creates copies in specific sizes based on the final size you select, chosen from among 3:2, 4:3, and 5:4 aspect ratios (proportions) (see Figure 4.12). You can use this feature to create smaller versions of a picture for e-mailing or uploading to Instagram without the need to first transfer the image to your own computer. If you're traveling, create your smaller copy here;

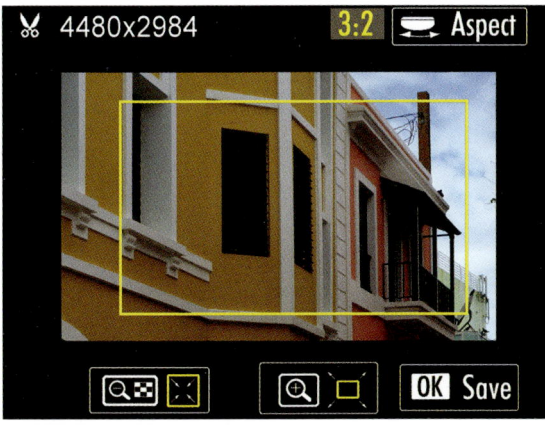

Figure 4.12
The Trim feature of the Retouch menu allows in-camera cropping.

insert the memory card in a card reader at an Internet café, your library's public computers, or some other computer; and e-mail the reduced-size version. Just follow these steps:

1. **Select your photo.** Choose Trim from the Retouch menu. You'll be shown the standard Nikon D5500 image selection screen. Scroll among the photos using the multi selector left/right buttons or touch screen, and tap or press OK when the image you want to trim is highlighted. While selecting, you can temporarily enlarge the highlighted image by pressing the Zoom In button.

2. **Choose your aspect ratio.** Rotate the command dial to change from 3:2, 4:3, 5:4, 1:1 (great for Instagram!), and 16:9 aspect ratios. These proportions happen to correspond to the proportions of common print sizes, including the two most popular sizes: 4 × 6 inches (3:2) and 8 × 10 inches (5:4). (See Table 4.7 for trim sizes.)

3. **Crop in on your photo.** Press the Zoom In button to crop in on your picture. The pixel dimensions of the cropped image at the selected proportions will be displayed in the upper-left corner. The current framed size is outlined in yellow.

Table 4.7 Trim Sizes

Aspect Ratio	Sizes Available
3:2	5760 × 3850, 5120 × 3416, 4480 × 2984, 3840 × 2560, 3200 × 2128, 2560 × 1704, 1920 × 1280, 1280 × 856, 960 × 640, 640 × 424
4:3	5328 × 4000, 5120 × 3840, 4480 × 3360, 3840 × 2880, 3200 × 2400, 2560 × 1920, 1920 × 1440, 1280 × 960, 960 × 720, 640 × 480
5:4	5008 × 4000, 4800 × 3840, 4208 × 3360, 3600 × 2880, 2992 × 2400, 2400 × 1920, 1808 × 1440, 1200 × 960, 896 × 720, 608 × 480
1:1	3840 × 3840, 3360 × 3360, 2880 × 2880, 2400 × 2400, 1920 × 1920, 1440 × 1440, 960 × 960, 720 × 720, 480 × 480
16:9	6016 × 3384, 5760 × 3240, 5120 × 2880, 4480 × 2520, 3840 × 2160, 3200 × 1800, 2560 × 1440, 1920 × 1080, 1280 × 720, 960 × 536, 640 × 360

4. **Move cropped area within the image.** Use the multi selector left/right and up/down buttons to relocate the yellow cropping border within the frame.

5. **Save the cropped image.** Select OK to save a copy of the image using the current crop and size, or press the Playback button to exit without creating a copy. Copies created from JPEG Fine, Normal, or Standard have the same Image Quality setting as the original; copies made from RAW files or any RAW+JPEG setting will use JPEG Fine compression.

Resize

Options: 2.5, 1.1, 0.6, 0.3, 0.1 megapixels

My preference: N/A

This tool creates smaller copies of the selected images. It can be applied while viewing a single image in full-frame mode (just press the *i* button while viewing a photo), or accessed from the Retouch menu (especially useful if you'd like to select and resize multiple images).

1. **Select images.** If accessing from the Retouch menu, you can choose to select multiple images, or jump directly to the following two steps.

2. **Choose Size.** Next, select the size for the finished copy, from 2.5M (1920 × 1280 pixels), 1.1M (1280 × 856 pixels), 0.6M (960 × 640 pixels), 0.3M (640 × 424 pixels), or 0.1M (320 × 216 pixels).

3. **Confirm.** Press OK to create your copy.

D-Lighting

Options: High, Normal, Low corrections

My preference: N/A

This option brightens the shadows of pictures that have already been taken. Once you've selected your photo for modification, you'll be shown side-by-side images with the unaltered version on the left, and your adjusted version on the right. Under Effect, choose from High, Normal, or Low corrections. Press or tap Zoom In to magnify the image, or Playback to Cancel. The camera may identify up to three human subjects as Portraits, and if you select the Portrait Subjects option, D-Lighting will be applied only to the people. (This feature does not work when you've selected Off for Auto Image Rotation in the Playback menu.) When you're happy with the corrected image on the right, compared to the original on the left, press or tap OK to save the copy to your memory card.

Quick Retouch

Options: High, Normal, Low

My preference: N/A

This option brightens the shadows of pictures that have already been taken. Once you've selected your photo for processing, use the multi selector left/right keys in the screen that pops up. The amount of correction that you select (High, Normal, or Low) will be applied to the version of the image shown at right. The left-hand version of the image shows the uncorrected version. While working on your image, you can press the Zoom In button to temporarily magnify the original photo.

Quick Retouch first applies D-Lighting, then brightens shadows, enhances contrast, and adds color richness (saturation) to the image. Press OK to create a copy on your memory card with the retouching applied.

Red-Eye Correction

Options: User settings

My preference: N/A

This Retouch menu tool can be used to remove the residual red-eye look that remains after applying the Nikon D5500's other remedies, such as the red-eye reduction lamp. (You can use the red-eye tools found in most image editors, as well.) Select a picture that was taken with flash (non-flash pictures won't be available for selection). After you've selected the picture to process, press/tap OK. The image will be displayed on the LCD. You can magnify the image with the Zoom In button, scroll around the zoomed image with the multi selector buttons, and zoom out with the Zoom Out button. While zoomed, you can cancel the zoom by pressing the OK button. When you are finished examining the image, press OK again. The D5500 will look for red-eye, and, if detected, create a copy that has been processed to reduce the effect. If no red-eye is found, a copy is not created.

Straighten

Options: Rotate

My preference: N/A

Use this to create a corrected copy of a crooked image, rotated by up to five degrees, in increments of one-quarter of a degree. Use the right directional button to rotate clockwise, and the left directional button to rotate counter-clockwise. Press OK to make a corrected copy, or the Playback button to exit without saving a copy.

Distortion Control

Options: Reduce barrel distortion, reduce pincushion distortion

My preference: N/A

This option produces a copy with reduced barrel distortion (a bowing out effect) or pincushion distortion (an inward-bending effect), both most noticeable at the edges of a photo. You can select Auto to let the D5500 make this correction, or use Manual to make the fix yourself visually. Use the right directional button to reduce barrel distortion and the left directional button to reduce pincushion distortion. In both cases, some of the edges of the photo will be cropped out of your image. Press OK to make a corrected copy, or the Playback button to exit without saving a copy. Note that Auto cannot be used with images exposed using the Auto Distortion Control feature described earlier in this chapter. Auto works only with type G and type D lenses, and does not work well with certain lenses, such as fisheye lenses and perspective control lenses.

Perspective Control

Options: Tilt image

My preference: N/A

This option, the first on the second page of the Retouch menu (see Figure 4.13), lets you adjust the perspective of an image, reducing the falling back effect produced when the camera is tilted to take in the top of a tall subject, such as a building. Use the multi selector buttons to "tilt" the image in various directions and visually correct the distortion.

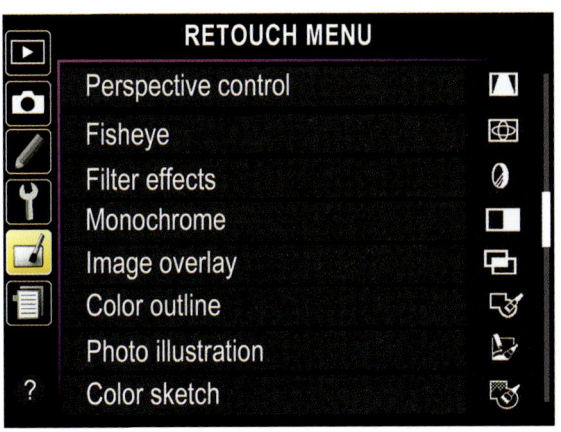

Figure 4.13

Perspective Control is the first entry on the second page of the Retouch menu.

Fisheye

Options: Increase, Decrease effect

My preference: N/A

This feature emulates the extreme curving effect of a fisheye lens. Use the right directional button to increase the effect, and the left directional button to decrease it. Press OK to make a corrected copy, or the Playback button to exit without saving a copy.

Filter Effects

Options: User Skylight, Warm, Red, Green, Blue, Cross Screen, Soft

My preference: N/A

Add tones to your images using this Retouch option. You have seven choices: Skylight, Warm, Red/Green/Blue intensifiers, Cross Screen, and Soft. Preview the effects in the color LCD before pressing OK to create the modified copy using the selected effect.

Monochrome

Options: B/W, Sepia, Cyanotype, Saturation

My preference: N/A

This Retouch choice allows you to produce a copy of the selected photo as a black-and-white image, sepia-toned image, or cyanotype (blue-and-white). You can fine-tune the color saturation of the previewed Sepia or Cyanotype version by pressing the multi selector up button to increase color richness, and the down button to decrease saturation. When satisfied, press OK to create the monochrome duplicate. Cancel by pressing the Playback button.

Image Overlay

Options: Merge two images

My preference: N/A

This feature allows you to combine two RAW photos (only NEF files can be used) in a composite image that Nikon claims is better than a "double exposure" created in an image-editing application, because the overlays are made using RAW data.

To produce this composite image, follow these steps:

1. **Choose Image Overlay in the Retouch menu.** The screen shown in Figure 4.14 will be displayed, with the Image 1 box highlighted.

2. **Select first image.** Press OK and the Nikon D5500's image selection screen appears. Highlight the first image for the overlay with the multi selector and press/tap OK to choose the photo and return to the preview display.

3. **Select second image.** Tap or Press the multi selector right button to highlight the Image 2 box, and press OK to produce the image selection screen. Choose the second image for the overlay.

4. **Adjust gain.** By highlighting either the Image 1 or Image 2 boxes and pressing the multi selector up/down buttons, you can adjust the "gain," or how much of the final image will be "exposed" from the selected picture. You can choose from X0.5 (half-exposure) to X2.0 (twice the exposure) for each image. The default value is 1.0 for each, so that each image will contribute equally to the final exposure.

5. **Examine combined image.** Use the multi selector right button to highlight the Preview box and view the combined picture. Press the Zoom In button to enlarge the view.

6. **Save new image.** When you're ready to store your composite copy, press the multi selector down button when the Preview box is highlighted to select Save, and press OK. The combined image is stored on the memory card.

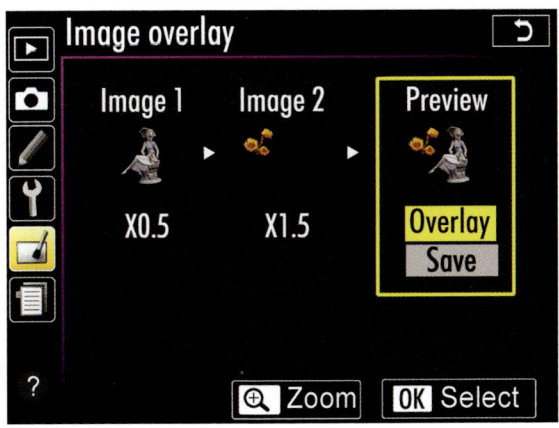

Figure 4.14
Overlay two RAW images to produce a "double exposure."

Color Outline

Options: Add Outline effect

My preference: N/A

This option creates a copy of your image in outline form, which Nikon says you can use for "painting." You might like the effect on its own. It's a little like the Find Edges command in Photoshop and Photoshop Elements, but you can perform this magic in your camera!

Photo Illustration

Options: Create pencil sketch effect

My preference: N/A

This option transforms your photo into a colored pencil sketch. Select Vividness or Outlines attributes, and the left/right buttons to increase/decrease saturation, or make the outlines thinner/thicker (respectively).

Color Sketch

Options: None

My preference: N/A

Adds a painterly effect to your images.

Miniature Effect

Options: Tilt/shift focus effect

My preference: N/A

This is the first entry on the last page of the Retouch menu (see Figure 4.15). This is a clever effect, and it's hampered by a misleading name and the fact that its properties are hard to visualize (which is not a great attribute for a visual effect). This tool doesn't create a "miniature" picture, as you might expect. What it does is mimic tilt/shift lens effects that angle the lens off the axis of the sensor plane to drastically change the plane of focus, producing the sort of look you get when viewing some photographs of a diorama, or miniature scene. Confused yet?

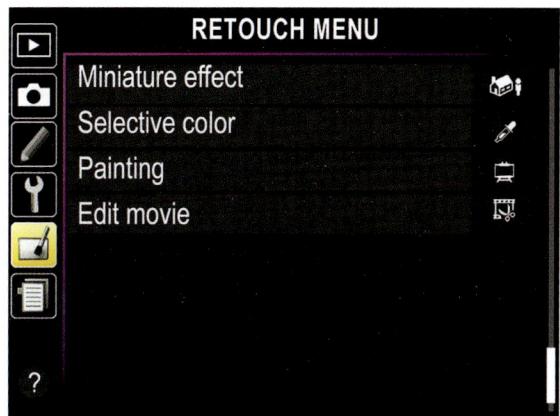

Figure 4.15
Miniature Effect is the first entry on the last page of the Retouch menu.

Perhaps the best way to understand this capability is to actually modify a picture using it. Just follow these steps:

1. **Take your best shot.** Capture an image of a distant landscape or other scene, preferably from a slightly elevated viewpoint.

2. **Access Miniature Effect.** When viewing the image during playback, press the *i* button to access the Retouch menu, and select Miniature Effect. A screen like the one shown in Figure 4.16, left, appears.

3. **Adjust selected area.** A wide yellow box (or a tall yellow box if the image is rotated to vertical perspective on playback) highlights a small section of the image. (No, we're not going to create a panorama from that slice; this Nikon super-tricky feature has fooled you yet again.) Use the up/down buttons (or left/right buttons if the image is displayed vertically) to move the yellow box, which represents the area of your image that will be rendered in (fairly) sharp focus. The rest of the image will be blurred.

4. **Preview area to be in sharp focus.** Press the Zoom In button to preview the area that will be rendered in sharp focus. Nikon labels this control Confirm, but that's just to mislead you. It's actually just a preview that lets you "confirm" that this is the area you want to emphasize.

5. **Apply the effect.** Press the OK button to apply the effect (or the Playback button to cancel). Your finished image will be rendered in a weird altered-focus way, as shown in Figure 4.16, right.

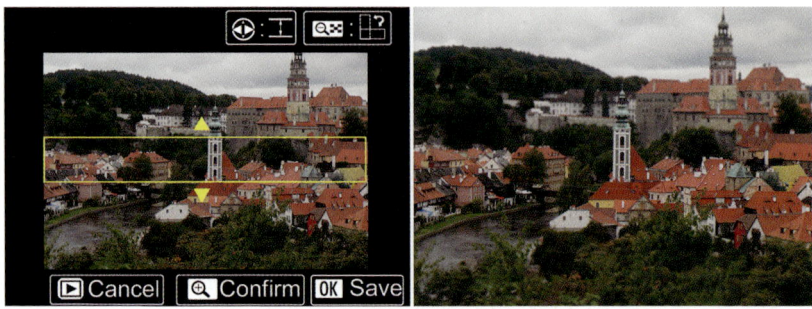

Figure 4.16 Choose the area for sharp focus by moving the yellow box within the frame (left). The same photo with the diorama/miniature effect applied (right).

Selective Color

Options: Specify color, range, tolerance

My preference: N/A

This is a retouching effect that allows you to choose which colors appear in a finished image, with the other colors rendered in black-and-white, resembling the effects seen in movies like *Sin City*, and every single wedding picture of a monochrome bride holding a vivid red rose. Your D5500 gives you access to this effect, to use creatively, or to reproduce some of the most popular clichés. To use it:

1. **Access Selective Color feature.** Choose Selective Color from the Retouch menu.

2. **Choose image.** When the Select Photo screen appears, highlight the one you want to process. You can preview the image in full frame by pressing the Zoom In button. When you've decided on the image, press the OK button. A screen like the one shown in Figure 4.17, left appears when you've chosen Selective Color from the menu.

3. **Specify a color.** Next, use the multi selector buttons to move the on-screen cursor over an area of the object with the color you want to specify and press the Protect/AF-L/AF-L button. The effect works best if you choose a rich, highly saturated color. You can enlarge a portion of the image by pressing the Zoom In button.

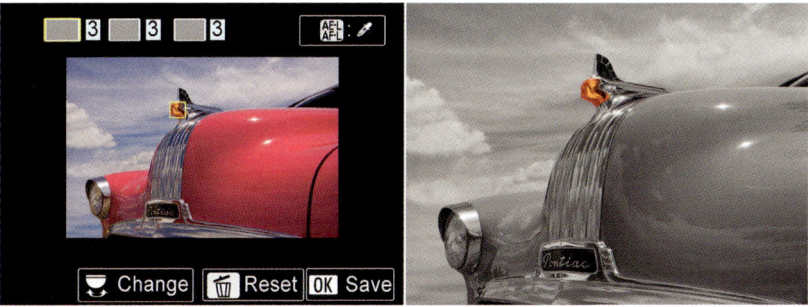

Figure 4.17 Select your colors and color ranges here (left). The finished effect looks like this (right).

4. **Add the selected color to a color range.** Rotate the command dial to choose one of the three color range boxes.

5. **Increase/decrease "tolerance."** Press the up/down multi selector buttons to increase or decrease the range of similar colors that will be included, with values from 1 to 7. A very broad range may extend the color selection into adjoining colors, say, embracing dark blues as well as lighter blues or even cyans.

6. **Choose a different color range box to add more colors.** Rotate the command dial again to highlight one of the other three color range boxes and repeat Steps 3 to 5 to add more colors.

7. **Save image.** Press OK to create a modified copy of your original photograph. (See Figure 4.17, right.)

Painting

Options: None

My preference: N/A

This effect exaggerates detail and color, producing a painterly effect. There are no options; just view the proposed version and either choose Cancel to exit or OK to save a copy using the effect.

Edit Movie

Options: User settings

My preference: N/A

You can edit movies as you view them, pausing (using the down directional button) and clipping off portions from the beginning and/or end of the movie to create an edited version. Movie editing can be done from this menu entry, or accessed by pausing and pressing the AE-L/AF-L button to display a retouching menu. I describe editing movies using this capability in detail in Chapter 6.

Side-by-Side Comparison

Options: User settings

My preference: N/A

Use this option to compare a previously retouched or copied photo side-by-side with the original from which it was derived. Don't look for Side-by-Side Comparison in the Retouch menu. It doesn't appear there. Instead, this option is shown at the bottom of the pop-up menu that appears when you are viewing an image (or copy) full screen and press the OK button.

To use Side-by-Side Comparison:

1. Press the Playback button and review images in full-frame mode until you encounter a source image or retouched copy you want to compare. The retouched copy will have the retouching icon displayed in the upper-left corner. Use the *i* button to select. Press OK.

2. The original and retouched image will appear next to each other, with the retouching options you've used shown as a label above the images.

3. Highlight the original or the copy with the multi selector left/right buttons, and press the Zoom In button to magnify the image to examine it more closely.

4. If you have created more than one copy of an original image, select the retouched version shown, and press the multi selector up/down buttons to view the other retouched copies. The up/down buttons will also let you view the other image used to create an Image Overlay copy.

5. When done comparing, press the Playback button to exit.

Using Special Effects Modes

Although the D5500's Special Effects modes are a type of Scene mode selection, I've elected to describe them here, because they are actually more closely related to the retouching effects we've explored in this chapter. Indeed, three of them are essentially identical, but are simply applied during shooting rather than after the image has already been captured.

To use Special Effects, set the mode dial to the EFFECTS position, and then rotate the command dial to cycle through the effects and select the one you want to use. Then, you can take pictures as always. However, when using Night Vision, Color Sketch, Miniature Effect, or Select Color special effects when RAW+JPEG has been selected for Image Quality, or if RAW (only) has been selected, only JPEG Fine images will be saved. No RAW image is created. The flash and AF-assist beam are disabled when using all these effects.

Your choices include:

- **Night Vision.** This effect gives you a monochrome image recorded at high ISO under very low light conditions. Because the light is so dim, autofocus is available only in Live View mode. You can use manual focus. The D5500's flash and AF-assist beam are disabled. You'll probably want to use a tripod, because this mode can use longer shutter speeds that accentuate camera movement. (See upper left, Figure 4.18.)
- **Super Vivid.** Increases the richness of the colors while boosting contrast.
- **Pop.** Boosts saturation like Super Vivid, but with less contrast.
- **Photo Illustration.** Like the Retouch feature with the same name, this setting sharpens outlines and reduces the number of colors in an image to create a poster-like effect. Unlike the Retouch version, you can adjust the settings as you preview the image in live view. Just press the OK button to display the options, and use the left/right buttons to make the poster outlines thicker or thinner. While this setting can be used in Movie mode, the clip plays back as a series of stills in a slide-show presentation.
- **Toy Camera Effect.** Take photos and movies with the low resolution and distortion typical of a toy camera. As with Photo Illustration, you can adjust the strength of the effect in live view.
- **Miniature Effect.** This setting produces the same look as the Miniature Effect retouching option described earlier in this chapter. I've seen some great video clips shot with this effect, making, in one example, Disneyland appear to be a miniature amusement park. No sound is recorded, but you can add your own audio later. The built-in flash and AF-assist beam are disabled.

- **Selective Color.** This setting creates an image with the selective color effects described previously. As with the other special effects, the built-in flash is disabled.
- **Silhouette.** Produces silhouettes against bright backgrounds, and flash is disabled. (See Figure 4.18, upper right.)
- **High Key.** Creates bright scenes. This effects tool, like the Low Key effect described next, can't work miracles. It won't produce a high-key image from a low-key subject. But if you have a scene that is filled with bright light, this effect will accentuate that, as seen at lower left in Figure 4.18.
- **Low Key.** Gives you dark, foreboding images. You'll need contrasty lighting to achieve this effect, but given the right subject, you can end up with an image like the one at lower right in Figure 4.18.

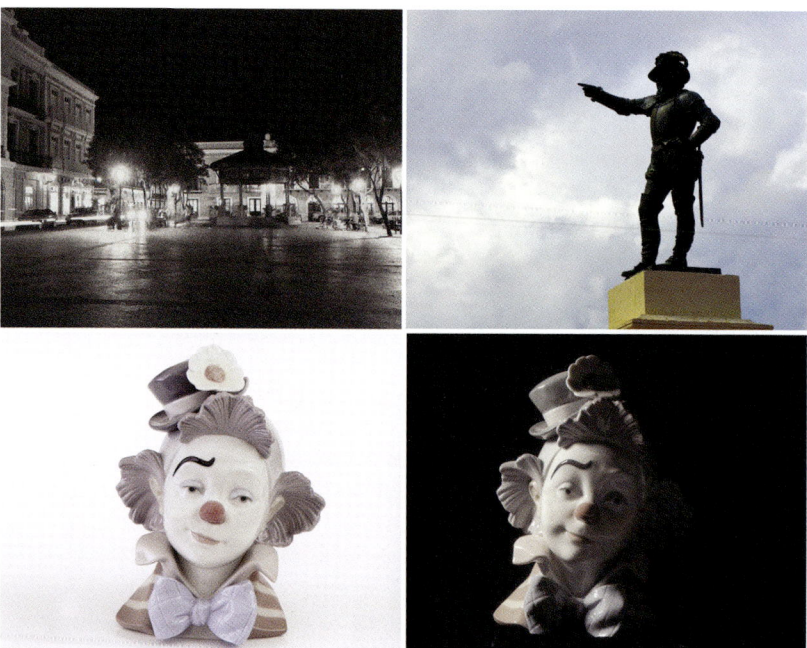

Figure 4.18 Special effects include Night Vision (upper left); Silhouette (upper right); High Key (lower left); and Low Key (lower right).

Using My Menu

The last menu in the D5500's main menu screen has two versions: Recent Settings and My Menu (see Figure 4.19). The default mode is Recent Settings, which simply shows an ever-changing roster of the 20 menu items you used most recently. You'll probably find it more useful to activate the My Menu option instead, which contains only those menu items that you deposit there.

Switching back and forth is easy. The My Menu and Recent Settings menus each has a menu choice called Choose Tab. Highlight that entry and press the right multi selector button to view a screen that allows you to activate either the My Menu or Recent Settings menu. Press OK to confirm.

You can add or subtract entries on My Menu at any time, and re-order (or rank) the entries so the ones you access most often are shown at the top of the list. Here's all you need to know to work with My Menu. To add entries to My Menu:

1. Select My Menu and choose Add Items.

2. A list of the available menus will appear (Playback, Shooting, Custom Setting, Setup, and Retouch menus). Highlight one and press the multi selector's right button.

3. Within the selected menu, choose the menu item you want to add and press OK.

4. The label Choose Position appears at the top of the My Menu screen. Use the up/down buttons to select a rank among the entries, and press OK to confirm and add the new item.

5. Repeat steps 1 to 4 if you want to add more entries to My Menu.

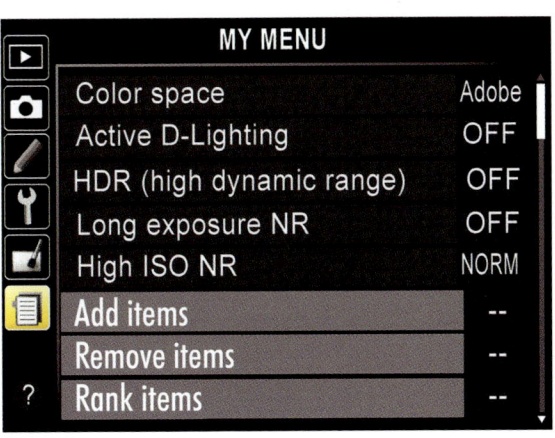

Figure 4.19
You can include your favorite menu items in the fast-access My Menu.

To reorder the menu listings:

1. Within the My Menu screen, choose Rank Items.
2. Use the up/down buttons to select the item to be moved, and press OK.
3. Use the up/down buttons to relocate the selected item and press OK.
4. Repeat steps 2 and 3 to move additional entries.

To remove entries from the list you can simply press the Trash button while an item is highlighted in the My Menu screen. To remove multiple items, follow these steps:

1. Within the My Menu screen, choose Remove Items.
2. A list with check boxes next to the menu items appears. Scroll down to an item you want to remove and press the multi selector right button to mark its box. If you change your mind, highlight the item and press the right button again to unmark the box.
3. When finished, highlight Done and press the OK button.
4. Press OK to confirm the deletion.

Chapter 5

Using the Flash

Your D5500 has a flip-up electronic flash unit built in, but you can also use an external flash (or, "strobe" or "Speedlight"), either mounted on the D5500's accessory shoe or used off-camera and linked with a cable or triggered by a slave light (which sets off a flash when it senses the firing of another unit's main flash). Consider using electronic flash:

- **When you need extra light.** Flash provides extra illumination in dark environments where existing light isn't enough for a good exposure, or is too imbalanced to allow a good exposure even with the camera mounted on a tripod.

- **When you don't need a precise preview of lighting effects.** Unless you're using a studio flash with a full-time modeling lamp, electronic flash works best when you are able to visualize its effects in your mind, or don't need a precise preview.

- **When you need to stop action.** The brief duration of electronic flash serves as a very high "shutter speed" when the flash is the main or only source of illumination for the photo. Your D5500's shutter speed may be set for 1/200th second during a flash exposure, but if the flash illumination predominates, the *effective* exposure time will be the 1/1,000th to 1/50,000th second or less duration of the flash, because the flash unit reduces the amount of light released by cutting short the duration of the flash. However, if the ambient light is strong enough, it may produce a secondary, "ghost" exposure, as I'll explain later in this chapter.

- **When you need flexibility.** Electronic flash's action-freezing power allows you to work without a tripod in the studio (and elsewhere), adding flexibility and speed when choosing angles and positions. Flash units can be easily filtered, and, because the filtration is placed over the light source rather than the lens, you don't need to use high-quality filter material.

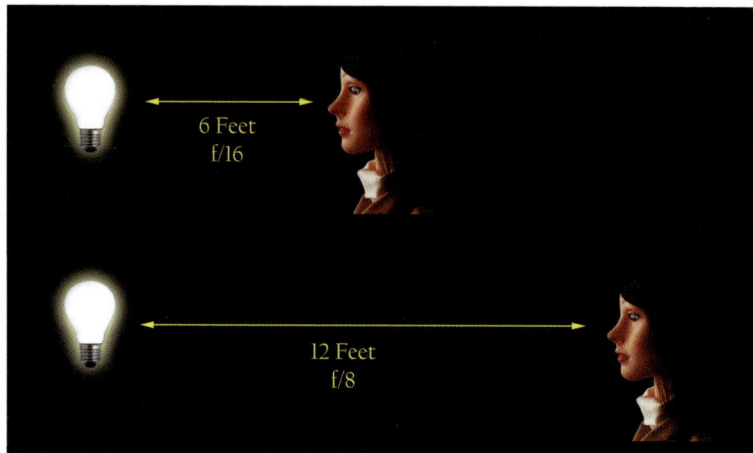

Figure 5.1 A light source that is twice as far away provides only one-quarter as much illumination.

■ **When you can use—or counter—flash's relatively shallow "depth-of-light" (the inverse square law).** Electronic flash units don't have the sun's advantage of being located 93 million miles from the subject, and suffer from the effects of their proximity. The *inverse square law* dictates that as a light source's distance increases from the subject, the amount of light reaching the subject falls off proportionately to the square of the distance. In plain English, that means that a flash or lamp that's 12 feet away from a subject provides only one-quarter as much illumination as a source that's 6 feet away (rather than half as much). (See Figure 5.1.) You can *use* this effect to separate subjects located at different distances thanks to the differing amount of illumination each receives. But when you want a larger area blanketed more evenly with illumination, you have to *counter* the effects of the inverse square law with supplemental lighting, slow shutter speeds (which allow ambient light to register along with the flash), bouncing the light off a ceiling or other surface to spread the light over a wider area, or by repositioning your subjects so all are within your flash's depth-of-light coverage.

Flash Control

The Nikon D5500's built-in flash has two modes, TTL and Manual. It does not have a repeating flash option, nor can it be used to trigger other Nikon flashes in Commander mode, unlike its siblings the Nikon D90 or Dxxx series, and above. You can choose between TTL and Manual modes using the Flash Control for Built-In Flash entry, Custom Setting e1 in the Custom menu, as first described in Chapter 4. Note that the label on this menu listing changes to Optional Flash when the SB-400 external flash is mounted on the D5500 and powered up. You can then make the same flash mode changes for the SB-400 as you can for the built-in flash. Other Nikon external flash units, such as the Nikon SB-910, have additional exposure modes, which I'll discuss later in this chapter. You'll want to consult the manual that came with your flash to see exactly which modes and options are available. Your Flash Control options are as follows:

- **TTL.** When the built-in flash is triggered, the D5500 first fires a pre-flash and measures the light reflected back and through the lens to calculate the proper exposure when the full flash is emitted a fraction of a second later.
- **Manual.** You can set the level of the built-in flash from full power to a fraction which, depending on the flash you are using, can range from 1/2 to 1/32, 1/64, or 1/128 power. A flash icon blinks in the viewfinder and on the shooting information display when you're using Manual mode, and the built-in flash has been flipped up.

Flash Metering Mode

You don't select the way your flash meters the exposure directly; the two modes, i-TTL Balanced fill flash and Standard i-TTL fill flash, are determined by the camera metering mode—Matrix, Center-weighted, or Spot—that you select.

- **i-TTL Balanced fill flash.** This flash mode is used automatically when you choose Matrix or Center-weighted exposure metering. The Nikon D5500 measures the available light and then adjusts the flash output to produce a natural balance between main subject and background. This setting is useful for most photographic situations.
- **Standard i-TTL fill flash.** This mode is activated when you use Spot metering or choose the standard mode with an external flash unit's controls. The flash output is adjusted only for the main subject of your photograph, and the brightness of the background is not factored in.

Choosing a Flash Sync Mode

The Nikon D5500 has five flash sync modes that determine when and how the flash is fired. They are selected from the information edit screen, or by holding down the flash button on the front of the camera lens housing while rotating the command dial. In both cases, the mode chosen appears in the information edit screen as the selection is made.

Not all sync modes are available with all exposure modes. Depending on whether you're using Scene modes, or Program, Shutter-priority, Aperture-priority, or Manual exposure modes, one or more of the following sync modes may not be available. I'm going to list the sync options available for each exposure mode separately, although that produces a little duplication among the options that are available with several exposure modes. However, this approach should reduce the confusion over which sync method is available with which exposure mode.

In Program and Aperture-priority modes, you can select these flash modes:

- **Fill flash.** In this mode (which uses front-curtain sync), represented by a lightning bolt symbol, the flash fires as soon as the front curtain opens completely. The shutter then remains open for the duration of the exposure, until the rear curtain closes. If the subject is moving and ambient light levels are high enough, the movement will cause a secondary "ghost" exposure that appears to be a stream of light advancing ahead of the flash exposure of the same subject.

- **Rear-curtain sync.** With this setting, the front curtain opens completely and remains open for the duration of the exposure. Then, the flash is fired and the rear curtain closes. If the subject is moving and ambient light levels are high enough, the movement will cause a secondary "ghost" exposure that appears to stream *behind* the flash exposure. In Program and Aperture-priority modes, the D5500 will combine rear-curtain sync with slow shutter speeds (just like slow sync, discussed below) to balance ambient light with flash illumination. (It's best to use a tripod to avoid blur at these slow shutter speeds.) (See Figure 5.2.)

- **Red-eye reduction.** In this mode, there is a one-second lag after pressing the shutter release before the picture is actually taken, during which the D5500's red-eye reduction lamp lights, causing the subject's pupils to contract (assuming they are looking at the camera), and thus reducing potential red-eye effects. Don't use with moving subjects or when you can't abide the delay.

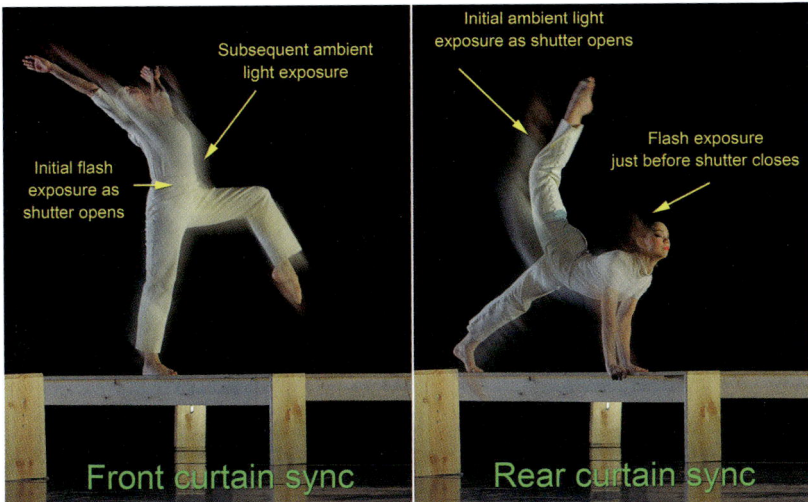

Figure 5.2 Front-curtain sync produces an image that trails in front of the flash exposure (left), while rear-curtain sync creates a more "natural looking" trail behind the flash image (right).

- **Slow sync.** This setting allows the D5500 in Program and Aperture-priority modes to use shutter speeds as slow as 30 seconds with the flash to help balance a background illuminated with ambient light with your main subject, which will be lit by the electronic flash. You'll want to use a tripod at slower shutter speeds, of course. It's common that the ambient light will be much warmer than the electronic flash's "daylight" balance, so, if you want the two sources to match, you may want to use a warming filter on the flash. That can be done with a gel if you're using an external flash like the SB-700 or SB-910, or by taping an appropriate warm filter over the D5500's built-in flash. (That's not a convenient approach, and many find the warm/cool mismatch not objectionable and don't bother with filtration.)

- **Red-eye reduction with slow sync.** This mode combines slow sync with the D5500's red-eye reduction behavior when using Program or Aperture-priority modes.

In Shutter-priority and Manual exposure modes, you can select the following three flash synchronization settings:

- **Front-curtain sync/Fill flash.** This setting should be your default setting. This mode is also available in Program and Aperture-priority mode, as described above, and, with high ambient light levels, can produce ghost images.

- **Red-eye reduction.** This mode, with its one-second lag and red-eye lamp flash, was described previously.

- **Rear-curtain sync.** As noted previously, in this sync mode, the front curtain opens completely and remains open for the duration of the exposure. Then, the flash is fired and the rear curtain closes. If the subject is moving and ambient light levels are high enough, the movement will cause that "ghost" exposure that appears to be trailing the flash exposure. (See Figure 5.2.)

In Auto, Portrait, Child, and Close Up modes, the following flash sync options are available:

- **Auto.** This setting is the same as front-curtain sync, but the flash pops up automatically in dim lighting conditions.

- **Red-eye reduction auto.** In this mode, there is a one-second lag after pressing the shutter release before the picture is actually taken, during which the D5500's red-eye reduction lamp lights, causing the subject's pupils to contract (assuming they are looking at the camera), and thus reducing potential red-eye effects. Don't use with moving subjects or when you can't abide the delay.

- **Flash off.** This is not really a sync setting, although it is available from the same selection screen. It disables the flash for those situations in which you absolutely do not want it to pop up and fire.

In Night Portrait mode, only slow synchronization flash and flash off modes are available:

- **Auto slow sync.** This setting allows the D5500 to select shutter speeds as slow as 30 seconds with the flash to help balance a background illuminated with ambient light with your main subject, which will be lit by the electronic flash. Best for shooting pictures at night when the subjects in the foreground are important, and you want to avoid a pitch-black background. I recommend using a tripod in this mode.

- **Auto red-eye reduction with slow sync.** Another mode that calls for a tripod, this sync setting mode combines slow sync with the D5500's red-eye reduction pre-flash. This is the one to use when your subjects are people who will be facing the camera.
- **Flash off.** Disables the flash in museums, concerts, religious ceremonies, and other situations in which you absolutely do not want it to pop up and fire.

Avoiding Sync Speed Problems

Using a shutter speed faster than 1/200th second can cause problems. To obtain shutter speeds faster than 1/200th second, the D5500 exposes only part of the sensor at one time, by starting the rear curtain on its journey before the front curtain has completely opened. That effectively provides a briefer exposure as a slit that's narrower than the full height of the sensor passes over the surface of the sensor. If the flash were to fire during the time when the first and second curtains partially obscured the sensor, only the slit that was actually open would be exposed, as shown in Figure 5.3. Fortunately, the camera prevents you from using speeds faster than 1/200th second in most cases. Even if you're shooting in Manual exposure mode, you'll find it impossible to choose a speed faster than 1/200th second. All bets are off if you're using a non-dedicated flash, such as a studio flash unit or an older electronic flash that uses a "dumb" PC/X connection. If you connect such a flash to the D5500 through a hot shoe adapter, the camera has no idea that a flash is connected to the camera, and will allow you to set a higher shutter speed, producing the effect shown in the figure.

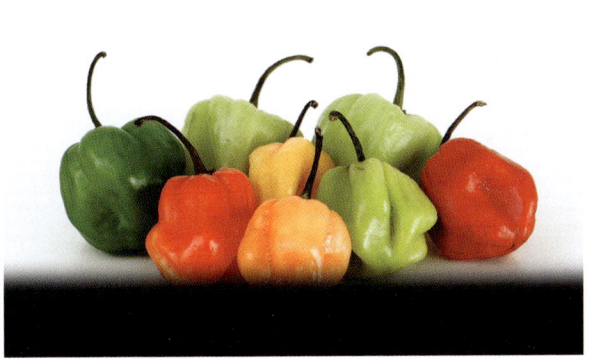

Figure 5.3
If a shutter speed faster than 1/200th second is used, you can end up photographing only a portion of the image.

Guide Numbers

Guide numbers, usually abbreviated GN, are a way of specifying the power of an electronic flash in a way that can be used to determine the right f/stop to use at a particular shooting distance and ISO setting. A GN is usually given as a pair of numbers for both feet and meters that represent the range at ISO 100. For example, the Nikon D5500's built-in flash has a GN in i-TTL mode of 12/39 (meters/feet) at ISO 100. In Manual mode, the true guide number is a fraction higher: 13/43 meters/feet. To calculate the right exposure at that ISO setting, you'd divide the guide number by the distance to arrive at the appropriate f/stop.

Using the D5500's built-in flash as an example, at ISO 100 with its GN of 43 in Manual mode, if you wanted to shoot a subject at a distance of 10 feet, you'd use f/4.3 (43 divided by 10), or, in practice, f/4.0. At 5 feet, an f/stop of f/8 would be used. Some quick mental calculations with the GN will give you any particular electronic flash's range. You can easily see that the built-in flash would begin to peter out at about 13 feet if you stuck to the lowest ISO of 100, because you'd need an aperture of f/2.8. Of course, in the real world you'd probably bump the sensitivity up to a setting of ISO 800 so you could use a more practical f/8 at 13 feet, and the flash would be effective all the way out to 20 feet or more at wider f/stops.

Working with Nikon Flash Units

If you want to work with dedicated Nikon flash units, at the time of this writing you have several choices: the D5500's built-in flash, the Nikon SB-910, SB-700, SB-500, the recently discontinued SB-400 flash units, the SB-300, and the SB-R200 wireless remote flash.

Nikon SB-300

This entry-level Speedlight, at about $150, is the smallest and most basic of the Nikon series of Speedlights. The SB-300 has a limited, easy-to-use feature set suited for point-and-shoot photography and some slightly more advanced techniques. Do note, however, that it does not support wireless off-camera flash. The SB-300 has a moderate guide number of 18/59 at ISO 100. Its main advantage, then, is to provide some additional elevation of the flash above the camera to provide an improved coverage angle and less chance of red-eye effects. Its flash head tilts up to 120 degrees, with click stops at 120, 90, 75, and 60 degrees when the flash is pointed directly ahead. It has a zoom flash head. The SB-300 is lighter in weight at 3.4 ounces than the SB-400 it replaces, and uses two AAA batteries.

Nikon SB-400

Recently discontinued, but still widely available new from many retailers, this entry-level Speedlight was, until the SB-300 was unveiled, the smallest and most basic of the series. The SB-400 has a limited, easy-to-use feature set suited for point-and-shoot photography and some slightly more advanced techniques. Do note, however, that like the SB-300, it does not support wireless off-camera flash. The 4.5-ounce SB-400 has a moderate guide number of 21/69 at ISO 100 when the zooming head (which can be set to either 18mm or 27mm) is at the 18mm position. It tilts up to 90 degrees, allowing you to bounce the light off of a ceiling, but it cannot be rotated to the side.

Nikon SB-500

This newest Nikon flash unit ($250) has a guide number of 24/79 at ISO 100, a speedy recycle time of about 3.5 seconds, and runs on 2 AA batteries for up to 140 flashes. It includes a built-in LED video light with three output levels. The SB-500's head tilts up to 90 degrees, with click-stops at 0, 60, 75, and 90. It rotates horizontally 180 degrees to the left and right, for flexible bounce-flash lighting. If you need a zoom head to adjust flash output to better distribute light at various focal lengths, you're better off with the SB-700 even with its limited zoom range (described next); this unit lacks zooming capabilities.

Nikon SB-700

This affordable (about $330) unit has a guide number of 28/92 (meters/feet) at ISO 100 when set to the 35mm zoom position. It has many of the top-model SB-910's features, including zoomable flash coverage equal to the field of view of a 16-56mm lens on the D5500 (24-120mm settings with a full-frame camera), and 14mm with a built-in diffuser panel. It has a built-in modeling flash feature, a wireless Commander mode, and automatic detection of DX format when mounted on non-FX camera models.

But the SB-700 lacks some important features found in the SB-910. Depending on how you use your Speedlight, these differences may or may not be important to you.

Most D5500 owners will not miss these capabilities:

- **No repeating flash mode.** You can't shoot interesting stroboscopic effects with the SB-700, as you can with the SB-910.

- **No port for external power pack.** Using an external battery pack, like those available from Quantum and others can be important for wedding and event photographers who want to fire off a bunch of shots quickly, while avoiding frequent changes of the AA batteries the SB-700 uses. An external pack has another benefit: more exposures before the Speedlight slows down to prevent overheating. External batteries don't generate heat inside the flash as internal batteries do.

- **Limited zoom range.** The SB-700's zoom head is limited. The ability to match the zoom head to the focal length you're using can match the coverage to the field of view, so the flash's output isn't wasted illuminating areas that aren't within the actual frame.

Nikon SB-R200

One oddball flash unit in the Nikon line is the SB-R200. This is a specialized wireless-only flash that's especially useful for close-up photography, and is often purchased in pairs for use with the Nikon R1 and R1C1 Wireless Close-Up Speedlight systems. Its output power is low at 10/33 (meters/feet) for ISO 100 as you might expect for a unit used to photograph subjects that are often inches from the camera. It has a fixed coverage angle of 78 degrees horizontal and 60 degrees vertical, but the flash head tilts down to 60 degrees and up to 45 degrees (with detents every 15 degrees in both directions). In this case, "up" and "down" has a different meaning, because the SB-R200 can be mounted on the SX-1 Attachment Ring mounted around the lens, so the pair of flash units are on the sides and titled toward or away from the optical axis. It supports i-TTL, D-TTL, TTL (for film cameras), and Manual modes.

Nikon SB-910

The Nikon SB-910 is currently the flagship of the Nikon flash lineup at around $550, and has a guide number of 34/111.5 (meters/feet) when the "zooming" flash head (which can be set to adjust the coverage angle of the lens) is set to the 35mm position. It has all the features of the D5500's built-in flash unit, including Commander mode.

Nikon estimates that you should be able to get 190 flashes from the SB-910 when using AA 2600 mAh rechargeable batteries, if firing the Speedlight at full output once every 30 seconds, with a minimum recycling time of 2.3 seconds (which gradually becomes longer as the flash heats up and the thermal protection kicks in). To get the maximum number of shots from your batteries, Nikon figures that AF-assist illumination, power zoom, and the LCD panel illumination are switched off.

The SB-910 also has its own powerful focus assist lamp to aid autofocus in dim lighting, and has reduced red-eye effects simply because the unit, even when attached to the D5500 and not used off-camera, is mounted in a higher position that tends to eliminate reflections from the eye back to the camera lens.

Using the Zoom Head

External flash zoom heads can adjust themselves automatically to match lens focal lengths in use reported by the D5500 to the flash unit, or you can adjust the zoom head position manually with some models. With flash units prior to the SB-900, automatic zoom adjustment wasted some of your flash's power, because the flash unit assumed that the focal length reported comes from a full-frame camera. Because of the 1.5X crop factor, the flash coverage when the flash is set to a particular focal length was wider than is required by the D5500's cropped image. The SB-900/910 and SB-700, on the other hand, automatically determine whether your camera is an FX-format, full-frame model, or is a DX ("cropped sensor") model like the Nikon D5500, and adjusts coverage angle to suit.

To set the zoom position manually, follow one of these steps:

- **SB-910.** Press the Function 1 button to select the Zoom function, and then rotate the selector dial to set the zoom head position. A clockwise turn increases the value, while counterclockwise rotation decreases the zoom setting. Alternatively, you can press the Function 1 button repeatedly to increase the zoom value; it will wrap around to the widest position once you reach the maximum. To restore Power Zoom operation, press the Function 1 button to display Zoom, then press the Function 2 button. An "M" appears on the LCD above the Zoom indicator to show that the zoom setting has been made manually. An FX or DX indicator appears to the left, just above the Zoom indicator to show that the SB-910 is set for FX or DX coverage.

- **SB-900.** Manually setting the zoom position is slightly different with the older SB-900 Speedlight. Press the Zoom button (located southwest of the selector dial/OK button pad) once, release it, and then rotate the selector dial until the zoom setting you want appears on the LCD. An "M" appears on the LCD above the Zoom indicator to show that the zoom setting has been made manually. An FX or DX indicator appears to the left, just above the Zoom indicator to show that the SB-900 is set for FX or DX coverage. You can also change the zoom setting by pressing the Zoom button repeatedly, in which case the focal length setting will jump from one increment to the next, wrapping around at 200mm back to the 12mm setting.

■ **SB-700.** Press the Zoom button to the left of the selector dial to highlight Zoom on the flash's LCD screen. Then, rotate the control dial to the zoom position you want. Press the center OK button on the selector dial to confirm your setting. (You can also cycle through the available zoom settings by pressing the Zoom button repeatedly.) An M appears above the Zoom indicator on the LCD to show you've set the zoom value manually. To switch back to power zoom, press the Zoom button until the power zoom icon appears (it's the word "zoom" with a back-looping arrow). Then press the SEL (Select) button to confirm.

Flash Modes

The TTL automatic flash modes available for the SB-900/910 and SB-700 are as follows: (The first three modes are not available with the SB-700.)

■ **AA.** Auto Aperture flash. The SB-900/910 uses a built-in light sensor to measure the amount of flash illumination reflected back from the subject, and adjusts the output to produce an appropriate exposure based on the ISO, aperture, focal length, and flash compensation values set on the D5500. This setting on the flash (available with the SB-900/910 only) can be used with the D5500 in Program or Aperture-priority modes.

■ **A.** Non-TTL auto flash. The SB-900's sensor measures the flash illumination reflected back from the subject, and adjusts the output to provide an appropriate exposure. This setting on the flash can be used when the D5500 is set to Aperture-priority or Manual modes. You can use this setting (available with the SB-900/910 only) to manually "bracket" exposures, as adjusting the aperture value of the lens will produce more or less exposure.

■ **GN.** Distance priority manual. You enter a distance value, and the SB-900 adjusts light output based on distance, ISO, and aperture to produce the right exposure in either Aperture-priority or Manual exposure modes. Press the MODE button on the flash until the GN indicator appears, then press the SEL button to highlight the distance display, using the plus and minus buttons to enter the distance value you want (from 1 to 65.6 feet, or 0.3 to 20 meters). The SB-900/910 will indicate a recommended aperture, which you then set on the lens mounted on the D5500.

- **M.** Manual flash. The flash fires at a fixed output level. Press the MODE button until M appears on the SB-900/910's LCD monitor panel. Press the SEL button and the plus or minus buttons to increase or decrease the output value of the flash. Use the table in the flash manual to determine a suggested aperture setting for a given distance. Then, set that aperture on the D5500 in either Aperture-priority or Manual exposure modes.

- **RPT.** Repeating flash. The flash fires repeatedly to produce a multiple flash strobing effect. To use this mode, set the D5500's exposure mode to Manual. Then set up the number of repeating flashes per frame, frequency, and flash output level on the SB-900/910.

Working with Wireless Commander Mode

The D5500's built-in flash cannot be set to Commander mode and used to control other compatible flash units. However, if you mount one of several compatible external dedicated flash units, such as the Nikon SB-500, it can serve as a flash "Commander" to communicate with and trigger other flash units. Nikon offers a unit called the SU-800, which is a commander unit that has no built-in visible flash, and which controls other units using infrared signals.

The SU-800 has several advantages. It's useful for cameras like the D5500, which lacks a Commander mode, and several "pro" cameras, like the D4, D3x, D3, and D2xs, which have no built-in flash to function in Commander mode. The real advantage the SU-800 has is its "reach." Because it uses IR illumination rather than visible light to communicate with remote flashes, the infrared burst can be much stronger, doubling its effective control range to 66 feet.

Once you have set the SB-500 or other flash as the Master/Commander, you can specify a shooting mode, either Manual with a power output setting you determine from 1/1 to 1/128, or for TTL automatic exposure. When using TTL, you can dial in from −1.0 to +3.0 flash exposure compensation for the master flash. You can also specify a channel (1, 2, 3, or 4) that all flashes will use to communicate among themselves. (If other Nikon photographers are present, choosing a different channel prevents your flash from triggering their remotes, and vice versa.)

Each remote flash unit can also be set to one of three groups (A, B, or C), so you can set the exposure compensation and exposure mode of each group separately. For example, one or more flashes in one group can be reduced in output compared to the flashes in the other group, to produce a particular lighting ratio or effect.

Connecting External Flash

You have three basic choices for linking an external flash unit to your Nikon D5500. They are as follows:

- **Mount on the accessory shoe.** Sliding a compatible flash unit into the Nikon D5500's accessory shoe provides a direct connection. With a Nikon dedicated flash, all functions of the flash are supported.

- **Connect to the accessory shoe with a cable or adapter.** The Nikon SC-28 and SC-29 TTL coiled remote cords have an accessory shoe on one end of a nine-foot cable to accept a flash, and a foot that slides into the camera accessory shoe on the other end, providing a link that is the same as when the flash is mounted directly on the camera. The SC-29 version also includes a focus assist lamp, like that on the camera and SB-900/910. You can also use an adapter in the accessory shoe that accepts a standard flash cable. In all cases, you should make sure that the external flash doesn't use a triggering voltage high enough to "fry" your camera's circuitry.

- **Wireless link.** Certain external Nikon electronic flash can be triggered by another Master flash such as the Nikon SB-700 or SB-900/910 in Commander mode or by the SU-800 infrared unit.

Using Flash Exposure Compensation

You can manually add or subtract exposure to the flash exposure calculated by the D5500. Just press the Flash button on the camera (just below the flash pop-up button) and rotate the command dial until the amount of exposure compensation you want appears in the viewfinder. You can make adjustments from –3 EV to +1 EV in 1/3 EV increments. As with ordinary exposure compensation, the adjustment you make remains in effect until you zero it out by pressing the Flash button and rotating the command dial until 0 appears on the monochrome control panel and in the viewfinder. To view the current flash exposure compensation setting, press the Flash button. When compensation is being used, an icon will be displayed in the viewfinder.

Chapter 6

Live View and Shooting Movies

The Nikon D5500 can shoot movies up to 4GB in size while the camera is in Live View mode. Shooting stills and movies in live view is easy. Before you start, you can check your settings, as described in the next section, or just forge ahead with the current settings by following the steps covered next.

Working with Live View

Activate live view by rotating the Lv switch on the top of the camera (just to the right of the mode dial) clockwise until the mirror flips up and the live view preview is shown on the display. The first thing to do when entering live view is to double-check the settings covered below that affect how your image or movie is taken.

Metering Mode

While using live view, you can press the *i* (information edit) button and use the information edit screen to select Matrix, Center-weighted, or Spot metering.

Focus Mode

Focus mode is chosen using the same information edit screen controls that apply when using the optical viewfinder.

- **AF-S.** This single autofocus mode, which Nikon calls single-servo AF, locks focus when the shutter release is pressed halfway and the focus frame is displayed in green. This mode uses *focus-priority;* the focus frame turns red and blinks if the camera is unable to achieve sharp focus.

■ **AF-F.** This new mode is roughly the equivalent of AF-C. Nikon calls it full-time servo AF. The D5500 focuses and refocuses continually as you shoot stills in live view or record movies. Unlike AF-C (which is not available in Live View or Movie modes), this mode also uses focus-priority. You can't release the shutter unless the camera has achieved sharp focus.

■ **MF.** Manual focus. You focus the image by rotating the focus ring on the camera.

Focus Area

Using the information edit screen, you can choose the focus area modes available, which are different from those used when working with the optical viewfinder. Your choices are as follows:

■ **Face-priority AF.** The camera automatically detects faces, and focuses on subjects facing the camera, as when you're shooting a portrait. You can't select the focus zone yourself. Instead, a double yellow border will be displayed on the LCD monitor when the camera detects a face. You don't need to press the shutter release to activate this behavior. (Up to 35 faces may be detected; the D5500 focuses on the face that is closest to the camera.) When you press down the shutter release halfway, the camera attempts to focus the face. As sharp focus is achieved, the border turns green. (See Figure 6.1.) If the camera is unable to focus, the border blinks red. Focus may also be lost if the subject turns away from the camera and is no longer detectable by Face-priority.

■ **Wide-area AF.** This is the mode to use for non-portrait subjects, such as landscapes, as you can select the focus zone to be used manually. It's good for shooting hand-held, because the subjects may change as you reframe the image with a hand-held camera, and the wide-area zones are forgiving of these changes. The focus zone will be outlined in red. You can move the focus zone around the screen with the multi selector buttons. When sharp focus is achieved, the focus zone box will turn green. (See Figure 6.2.)

■ **Normal-area AF.** This mode uses smaller focus zones, and so is best suited for tripod-mounted images where the camera is held fairly steady. As with Wide-area AF, the focus zone will be outlined in red. You can move the focus zone around the screen with the multi selector buttons. When sharp focus is achieved, the focus zone box will turn green. (See Figure 6.3.)

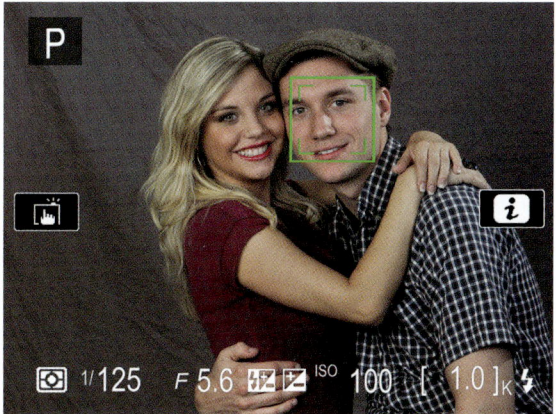

Figure 6.1
Face-priority AF attempts to focus on the face that's closest to the camera.

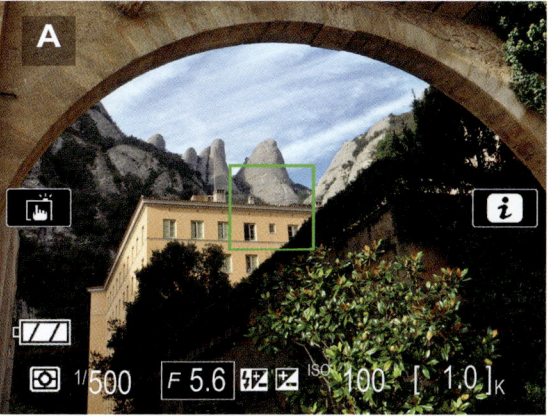

Figure 6.2
Wide-area AF is best for landscapes and other subjects with large elements.

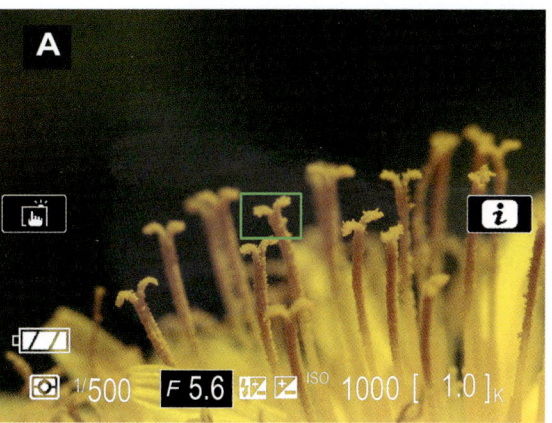

Figure 6.3
Normal-area AF allows you to zero in on a specific point of focus, such as the elements of this dandelion.

- **Subject-tracking AF.** This mode allows the camera to "grab" a subject, focus, and then follow the subject as it moves within the frame. You can use this mode for subjects that don't remain stationary, such as small children. When using Subject-tracking AF, a white border appears in the center of the frame, and turns green when focus is locked in (as described in the section that follows). To activate focus or refocus, press the multi selector OK button. I'll explain Subject-tracking in more detail next. (See Figure 6.4.)

- **Manual focus.** Set the lens focus-mode switch to M and the D5500's focus mode to Manual. Then, in this non-automatic focus mode, you can move the focus area around the frame with the multi selector buttons, (you can press the Zoom In button to magnify the image to make focusing easier) and then adjust focus manually by rotating the focus ring on the lens. When sharp focus is achieved, the red focus zone box will turn green, and the camera's beeper, if enabled, will sound.

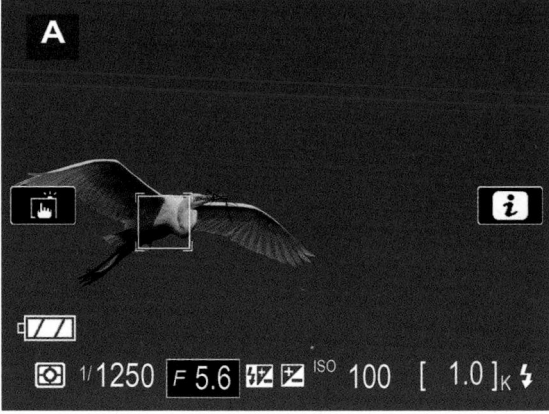

Figure 6.4
Subject-tracking AF can keep focus as it follows your subject around in the frame.

Subject-Tracking

Here's the quick introduction you need to Subject-tracking.

- **Ready, aim, …** When you've activated Subject-tracking, a white border appears in the center of the frame. Use that border to "aim" the camera until the subject you want to focus on and track is located within the border.

■ **…focus.** When you've pinpointed your subject, press the OK button to activate the D5500's contrast detection autofocus feature. The focus frame will turn yellow and the camera will emit a beep (unless you've disabled the beep with in the Setup menu) when locked in.

■ **Reframe as desired.** Once the focus frame has turned yellow, it seemingly takes on a life of its own, and will "follow" your subject around on the LCD monitor as you reframe your image. (See Figure 6.4.) (In other words, the subject being tracked doesn't have to be in the center of the frame for the actual photo.) Best of all, if your subject moves, the D5500 will follow it and keep focus as required.

■ **Tracking continues.** The only glitches that may pop up might occur if your subject is small and difficult to track, or is too close in tonal value to its background, or if the subject approaches the camera or recedes sufficiently to change its relative size on the LCD monitor significantly.

■ **Grab a new subject.** If you want to refocus or grab a new subject, press the OK button again.

AUTOMATIC SCENE SELECTION

If you have set the mode dial to Auto or Auto (Flash Off) when you switch to live view, and you are not using manual focus, the D5500 will analyze the scene and may switch to another Scene mode that's more appropriate for the scene. It may choose Portrait, Landscape, Close Up (if the subject is close to the camera), or Night Portrait (if the D5500 detects a dark background) Scene modes. If none of these seem especially suitable, the camera will fall back to Auto or Auto (Flash Off).

Viewing Live View Information

Once you've activated live view, a display like the one shown in Figure 6.5 appears. Not all of the information appears all the time. The indicators on the image can be displayed or suppressed by pressing the Info button (that's the one on the top of the camera, southwest of the shutter release). As you press the Info button on top of the camera repeatedly (not the *i* on the back to the right of the LCD monitor), the LCD monitor cycles among full information, minimal information, a screen with 16:9 HD movie aspect ratio indicated, or basic information with a 16-segment alignment grid.

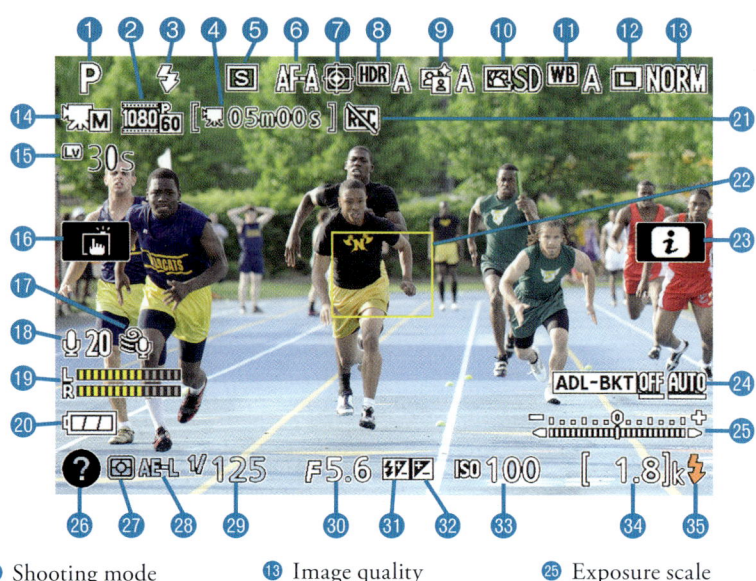

1. Shooting mode
2. Movie frame size
3. Flash mode
4. Movie time remaining
5. Release mode
6. AF mode
7. AF-area mode
8. HDR settings
9. Active D-Lighting status
10. Picture Control
11. White balance
12. Image size
13. Image quality
14. Manual movie settings
15. Time remaining
16. Touch shutter
17. Wind noise reduction
18. Microphone sensitivity
19. Sound level
20. Battery status
21. No movies possible
22. Focus point
23. Information edit
24. Bracketing
25. Exposure scale
26. Help
27. Metering mode
28. Autoexposure lock
29. Shutter speed
30. Aperture
31. Flash compensation
32. Exposure compensation
33. ISO
34. Exposures remaining
35. Flash mode

Figure 6.5 The live view display includes a lot of information, some of which can be hidden.

The overlaid indicators include:

- **Shooting mode.** This indicator shows the mode dial position you've selected, including any of the PASM (Program, Aperture-priority, Shutter-priority, and Manual) modes, as well as one of the Scene modes. You can change modes while live view is active. This indicator appears on the LCD monitor even when shooting information is turned off.

- **Sound level.** Shows when a microphone is being used. Microphone sensitivity and wind noise options are also available.

- **No movies possible.** This shows that it is not possible to shoot movies, because there is not enough space remaining on your memory card.

- **Live view time remaining.** This is displayed when the amount of shooting time in live view is 30 seconds or less. Although live view is possible for no more than 30 minutes, if the D5500 overheats, this countdown display appears and the camera exits live view before damage is done.

- **Flash mode.** Displays the flash mode.

- **Release mode.** Shows the current release mode.

- **Picture Control.** Currently selected Picture Control.

- **AF mode.** Shows AF-S, AF-F, or M focus.

- **AF-area mode.** Shows whether Face-priority, Wide-area, Normal-area, or Subject-tracking autofocus will be used. This indicator still appears when the alignment grid is displayed, even when other shooting information is turned off.

- **HDR settings.** Displayed when HDR mode is active.

- **Active D-Lighting status.** Shows the D-Lighting that will be applied.

- **Focus point.** Shows the appropriate focus indicator for the AF-area mode in use.

- **Image size.** Displays the current resolution, L (Large), M (Medium), or S (Small).

- **Image quality.** Shows JPEG image quality: Fine, Norm, or Basic.

- **White balance.** Displays the current white balance preset or WB Auto.

- **Movie time remaining.** Indicates the number of minutes and seconds remaining for movie shooting.

- **Movie frame size.** Displays the resolution of the movie frame and frames per second rate, from 1920 × 1080 pixels to 1280 × 720, down to 640 × 424, at either 24 or 30 fps (depending on what you've selected in the Movie Settings entry in the Shooting menu).

- **Alignment grid.** This set of guides can be used to help line up horizontal or vertical lines.
- **Battery status.** Current power level of the battery.

Additional information appears on the LCD monitor image, more or less duplicating much of the data in the LED display that is seen through the viewfinder, including metering method, shutter speed, f/stop, ISO value, and shots remaining.

Live View Exposure

Your D5500 will do an excellent job of adjusting exposure for you in any of the semi-automatic modes (Program, Aperture-priority, or Shutter-priority), as well as Scene modes and Special Effects modes when using live view.

- **Semi-automatic modes.** Rotate the mode dial to the mode you want (P, A, S) prior to capture, whether in live view or non–live view. To add or subtract exposure, hold down the EV button (just southeast of the shutter release) and rotate the main command dial to increase or reduce exposure. The back-panel color LCD monitor will brighten or darken to represent the exposure change you make.
- **Scene modes.** Use the dedicated mode dial positions to the Scene position and rotate the command dial to select any of the scenes. Press OK to confirm (or, if you pause for a few seconds, the D5500 will activate your choice and return to the shooting information screen). Note that you can select a Scene mode even if the shooting information screen is not currently displayed (press Info to display/hide it), and even if you have already entered live view.
- **Effects modes.** You can select a Special Effects mode exactly as you do a Scene mode, except that the mode dial needs to be rotated to the EFFECTS position. Just rotate the command dial to choose a Special Effect from the screen that pops up.
- **Manual exposure.** With the mode dial set to M, you can select shutter speed and aperture in Live View mode. Rotate the command dial to change the shutter speed; hold down the Exposure Compensation/ Aperture button (located south west of the shutter release) to adjust the aperture. The brightness of the LCD monitor does not change to provide an indication of the resulting exposure. **Note:** If you have activated Manual Movie Settings you will not be able to choose a shutter speed slower than 1/60th or 1/30th second in live view—even if you have no plans to capture video. I'll explain why in the next section.

Shooting in Live View

Shooting stills and movies in live view is easy. Just follow these steps:

1. **Rotate Lv switch.** Activate live view by rotating the switch on top of the camera. The D5500 can be hand-held or mounted on a tripod. (Using a tripod mode makes it easier to obtain and keep sharp focus.) You can exit live view at any time by rotating the Lv button again. It's a momentary contact switch that springs back to its original position when you release it.

2. **Automatic scene selection.** You can choose P, S, A, M, or one of the Scene modes manually, but if you choose Auto or Auto (Flash Off), the D5500 will analyze the scene and choose a mode for you automatically, choosing from Portrait, Landscape, Close Up, Night Portrait, or, if none of those apply, it will use the default Auto or Auto (Flash Off) settings.

3. **Zoom in/out.** Check your view by pressing the Zoom In and Zoom Out buttons (located to the right of the color LCD monitor). Ten levels of magnification are available, up to 33X zoom. A navigation box appears in the lower right of the LCD monitor with a yellow box representing the portion of the image zoomed, just as when you're reviewing photos you've already taken using Playback mode. Use the multi selector keys or a swipe on the touch screen to change the zoomed area within the full frame. Press the Zoom Out button to zoom out again.

4. **Make exposure adjustments.** While using an automatic exposure mode, you can add or subtract exposure using the EV settings, as described in Chapter 4, and in the next section.

5. **Shoot.** Press the shutter release all the way down to take a still picture, or press the red Movie button to start motion picture filming. Stop filming by pressing the Movie button again. Movies up to 4GB in size can be taken (assuming there is sufficient room on your memory card), which limits you to 20 minutes for an HDTV clip. If Touch Shutter is enabled, you can take a still photography by tapping the touch screen.

Shooting Movies with the D5500

Movie making is an extension of the live view concept. All the focus modes and AF-area modes described for Live View mode can be applied to movie making.

- **Stills, too.** You can take a still photograph even while you're shooting a movie clip by pressing the shutter release all the way down. You won't miss a still shot because you're shooting video. However, movie shooting will cease after you take the still, and must be re-activated by pressing the red Movie button again.

- **Exposure compensation.** When shooting movies, exposure compensation is available in plus/minus 3 EV steps in 1/3 EV increments.

- **Size matters.** Individual movie files can be no more than 4GB in size (this will vary according to the resolution you select), and no more than 20 minutes in length. The speed and capacity of your memory card may provide additional restrictions on size/length.

NOT MUCH OF A LIMITATION

Unless you are shooting an entire performance from a fixed position, such as a stage play, the 20-minute limitation on HDTV movie duration won't put much of a crimp in your style. Good motion picture practice calls for each production to consist of a series of relatively *short* clips, with 10 to 20 seconds a good average. You can assemble and edit your D5500 movies into one long, finished production using one of the many movie-editing software packages available. Andy Warhol might have been successful with his 1963 five-hour epic *Sleep*, but the rest of us will do better with short sequences of the type produced by the Nikon D5500.

In the Movie Settings entry of the Shooting menu, you can make the following choices:

- **Movie quality.** Choose your resolution. Use the Movie Settings entry in the Shooting menu. Or, when live view is activated, and before you start shooting your video clip, you can select the resolution/frame rate of your movie. All use *progressive scan,* in which all the lines are captured one after another in order. Your choices are as follows:
  - 1920 × 1080 at 60 fps, progressive scan (60p)
  - 1920 × 1080 at 30 fps, progressive scan (30p)
  - 1920 × 1080 at 24 fps, progressive scan (24p)
  - 1280 × 720 at 60 fps, progressive scan (60p)
  - 640 × 424 at 30 fps, progressive scan (30p). (Useful for video clips displayed on web pages.)

- **Movie quality.** Choose High quality (to capture up to 20 minutes of action) or Normal quality (for up to 29 minutes, 59 seconds of video per clip). The High setting has a maximum bit rate requirement of 24 Mbps; if your memory card won't handle that, the Normal setting reduces the demand to 12 Mbps, at the cost of some additional compression that reduces the size of the file and cuts resolution/image quality slightly.

- **Microphone.** Here you can set audio sensitivity for the built-in stereo microphones or an optional external mic like the Nikon ME-1 or ME-W1 wireless microphone. Choose from Auto, High Sensitivity, Medium Sensitivity, Low Sensitivity, or Off. With the Manual Sensitivity setting, a set of volume unit (VU) meter bars appears on the menu screen above showing the current sound levels. Press the right directional button to access a screen where you can select a manual sensitivity level from 1 to 20.

- **Wind noise reduction.** Gusts of wind can interfere with clear recording of your desired audio, so this option allows you to turn a built-in wind noise reduction feature on or off. In quiet surroundings you'll want to disable the feature, as it can clip off some audio frequencies that you may want to capture.

- **Manual movie settings.** Select On if you'd like to be able to adjust shutter speed and ISO sensitivity when shooting movies in the Manual exposure mode. Select Off if you won't need this capability, which is explained in the next section.

To shoot your movies, follow these steps, which are similar to those for using live view:

1. **Plug in microphone.** If you want to use an external monaural or stereo microphone with a 3.5mm stereo mini plug, attach it to the microphone jack on the left side of the camera.

2. **Start live view.** Activate live view by rotating the Lv switch.

3. **Choose a focus mode.** Select from AF-S, AF-F, or M, as described earlier.

4. **Choose an AF-area mode.** Choices include Face-priority AF, Wide-area AF, Normal-area AF, Subject-tracking AF, or Manual focus, as described earlier.

5. **Activate and lock in focus.** This was also described under the live view instructions.

6. **Preview framing.** If you want to preview the image area that will be captured when shooting video, you can press the Info button (the one *on top* of the camera) to show movie indicators. During actual capture, the movie frame area will be enlarged to fill the LCD monitor, so what you see is what you get.

7. **Start/Stop recording.** Press the red Movie button. Press again to stop recording.

Movie Exposure

Exposure in Movie mode is much the same as in Live View mode. You can use Manual exposure, any of the semi-automatic modes (Program, Aperture-priority, or Shutter-priority), as well as Scene modes and Special Effects modes (capturing video in Special Effects modes can produce some particularly inventive movie "looks").

- **Semi-automatic modes.** As in live view, just rotate the mode dial to the mode you want (P, A, S) prior to capture, whether in live view or non–live view modes. You can change to another mode while capturing video, but the recording will be interrupted and you'll need to press the Movie button again.

- **Scene modes.** Use the mode dial to select the Scene mode position. Rotate the control dial to choose your Scene mode. A screen will pop up showing each of the non-dial modes. Press OK to confirm (or, pause for a few seconds, and the D5500 will activate your choice). If you change Scene modes while capturing video, the recording will be interrupted and you'll need to press the Movie button again.

■ **Special Effects modes.** You can select a Special Effects mode exactly as you do a Scene mode, except that the mode dial needs to be rotated to the EFFECTS position. Just rotate the control dial to choose a Special Effect from the screen that pops up.

■ **Manual exposure.** With the mode dial set to M, and Manual Movie Settings activated in the Movie Settings entry of the Shooting menu, you can select shutter speed and aperture while shooting movies. If your D5500 is set for a "forbidden" shutter speed prior to activating Movie mode, the camera will automatically adjust to an appropriate speed.

The option to increase the shutter speed to a shorter value can be useful when capturing action and you don't want individual frames to have too much blur. Your best bet is to use a shutter speed that is about twice the frame rate—for example 1/60th second when shooting at 24 fps or 30 fps, and 1/125th second at 60 fps. You can up the speed a notch—say, 1/125th at 24/30 fps or 1/260th at 60 fps. However, using a *much* higher shutter speed, while freezing action, may make your images look jittery and unrealistic. The ability to adjust ISO settings manually allows you to compensate for the higher shutter speeds used, if necessary.

In all cases, however, your shutter speed range is limited to 1/4000th second at the high end, and no slower than 1/30th second at 30/24 fps rates or no slower than 1/60th second at 60 fps. ISO sensitivity can be chosen from ISO 100 to 25600.

Viewing Your Movies

Film clips show up during picture review, the same as still photos, but they are differentiated by a movie camera icon overlay. Press the OK button to start playback, then use these functions:

■ **Pause.** Press the multi selector down button to pause the clip during playback. Press the multi selector center button to resume playback.

■ **Rewind/Advance.** Rotate the command dial left or right to skip back or forward by 10 seconds.

■ **Single frame rewind/Advance.** Press the multi selector down key to pause the clip, then use the left/right buttons to rewind or advance one frame at a time.

■ **Change volume.** Press the Zoom In and Zoom Out buttons to increase/decrease volume.

■ **Trim movie.** Press the AE-L/AF-L button while the movie is paused. If you press the button before pausing, it simply adds the Protect attribute to the clip. You must first pause the movie to access the editing features.

- **Exit playback.** Press the multi selector up button or press the shutter release halfway to exit playback.
- **View menus.** Press the MENU button to interrupt playback to access menus.

Editing Movies

You can trim the beginning or ending from any clip that's at least two seconds long. For more advanced editing, you'll need an application capable of editing AVI movie clips. (Google "AVI Editor" to locate any of the hundreds of free video editors available, or use a commercial product like Corel Video Studio, Adobe Premiere Elements, or Pinnacle Studio.) To edit in-camera:

1. **Start movie clip.** Use the Playback button to start image review, and press OK when the LCD monitor shows a clip you want to edit. It will begin playing.

2. **Activate edit.** To remove video from the beginning of a clip, view the movie until you reach the first frame you want to keep, and then press the down button to pause. If the exact point you want to mark is not displayed, you can use the left/right directional buttons to advance or back up frames, or rotate the control dial to advance or back up 10 seconds at a time.

3. **Access edit screen.** Press or tap the information edit (*i*) button/icon to display the Edit Movie prompt. (See Figure 6.6.)

4. **Select start/end point.** Highlight the Choose Start/End Point option and press the right directional button. A screen appears asking whether you want to mark the current frame as the start or end point. Keep in mind that all frames *prior* to the pause will be deleted if you're in Choose Start Point mode; all frames *after* the pause will be deleted if you're in Choose End Point mode. Your trimmed movie must be at least two seconds long.

   - **Delete from beginning.** To remove video from the beginning of the clip, when you've reached the point where you want the video to commence, select Start Point to delete all the video that has been displayed prior to when you pressed pause.

   - **Delete at end.** To delete video from the end of the clip, advance to the last frame you want to use and select End Point. (As mentioned, the video that remains after trimming must always be at least two seconds long.) Press OK to confirm, or the Playback button to cancel the edit.

   Note: After you choose Select Start/End Point, you can still define the current frame as the Start or End Point by pressing the AE-L/AF-L button.

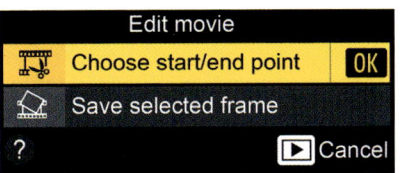

Figure 6.6
Choose editing options from this menu.

5. **Save edited clip.** When you've marked the beginning or end points, press the up directional button. A screen appears offering four choices, which you can highlight with the up/down directional buttons and activate with OK:

■ **Save as new file.** Your video clip will be stored under a different file name (but with the same time and date as the original clip), leaving the original movie untouched. Keeping the time/date stamp helps you determine when the video was originally captured, even if you are editing it at a later time.

■ **Overwrite existing file.** Your video clip will be stored using the same file name, time, and date, and the portion edited out will be lost. Use this option when you are certain that you do want to delete frames (say, you jerked the camera by accident at the beginning or end of the clip).

■ **Cancel.** Abandon the current editing and return to Step 4.

■ **Preview.** Displays the edited version of your clip.

6. **Save movie.** If you elect to save as a new file, or overwrite an existing file, you'll see a Saving Movie message and a progress bar as the D5500 stores the trimmed clip to your memory card. Storage takes some time, and you don't want to interrupt it to avoid losing your saved clip. So, make sure your camera has a fully charged battery before you start to edit a clip.

Saving a Frame

You can store any frame from one of your movies as a JPEG still, using the resolution of the video format. Just follow these steps:

1. Pause your movie at the frame you want to save. Press the *i* button to access the Edit Movie screen.

2. Choose Save Selected Frame and press OK.

3. Press the up button to choose Proceed and confirm.

4. Your frame will be stored on the memory card, and will be marked with a scissors icon.

Tips for Shooting Better Movies

There are a number of different things to consider when planning a video shoot.

Make a Shooting Script

A shooting script is nothing more than a coordinated plan that covers both audio and video and provides order and structure for your video. A detailed script will cover what types of shots you're going after, what dialogue you're going to use, audio effects, transitions, and graphics. A storyboard is a series of panels providing visuals that help you picture locations, placement of actors/actresses, props, and furniture. It also helps show how you want to frame or compose a shot. (See Figure 6.7.)

Advance a Story

A lot of the work will come after you shoot, when your video is assembled using a movie-editing program like iMovie or Windows Movie Maker. Audio and video should always be advancing the story. While it's okay to let the camera linger from time to time, it should only be for a compelling reason and only briefly. It only takes a second or two for an establishing shot to impart the necessary information, and the same goes for a dramatic stare. Provide variety too. Change camera angles and perspectives often and never leave a static scene on the screen for a long period of time.

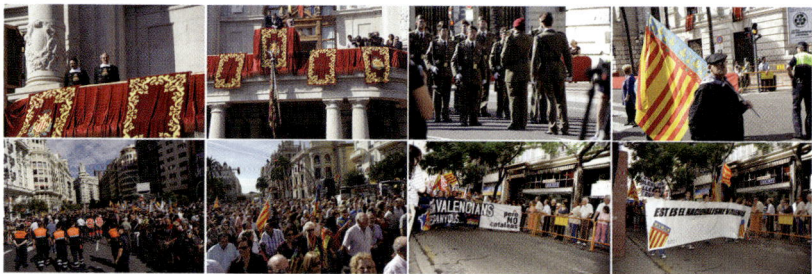

Figure 6.7 A storyboard is a series of simple sketches or photos to help visualize a segment of video.

Keep Transitions Basic

Fancy transitions that involve exotic "wipes," dissolves, or cross fades take too long for the average viewer and make your video ponderous. Save dissolves to show the passage of time (it's a cinematic convention that viewers are used to and understand).

Composition

Movie shooting calls for careful composition, and, in the case of HD video format, that composition must be framed by the 16:9 aspect ratio of the format. Static shots where the camera is mounted on a tripod and everything's shot from the same distance are a recipe for dull videos. Try these tricks:

- **Establishing shot.** This composition, shown at top left in Figure 6.8, establishes the scene and tells the viewer where the action is taking place.

- **Medium shot.** This shot is composed from about waist to headroom (some space above the subject's head). It's useful for providing variety from a series of close-ups and also makes for a useful first look at a speaker. (See Figure 6.8, top right.)

- **Close-up.** The close-up, usually described as "from shirt pocket to head room," provides a good composition for someone talking directly to the camera. (See Figure 6.8, middle left.)

- **Extreme close-up.** This shot has been described as the "big talking face" shot. Styles and tastes change over the years and now the big talking face is much more commonly used (maybe people are better looking these days?) and so this view may be appropriate. (See Figure 6.8, middle right.)

- **"Two" shot.** A two shot shows a pair of subjects in one frame. They can be side by side or one in the foreground and one in the background. Subjects can be standing or seated. A "three shot" is the same principle except that three people are in the frame. (See Figure 6.8, bottom left.)

- **Over-the-shoulder shot.** Long a tool of interview programs, the "over-the-shoulder shot" uses the rear of one person's head and shoulder to serve as a frame for the other person. This puts the viewer's perspective as that of the person facing away from the camera. (See Figure 6.8, bottom right.)

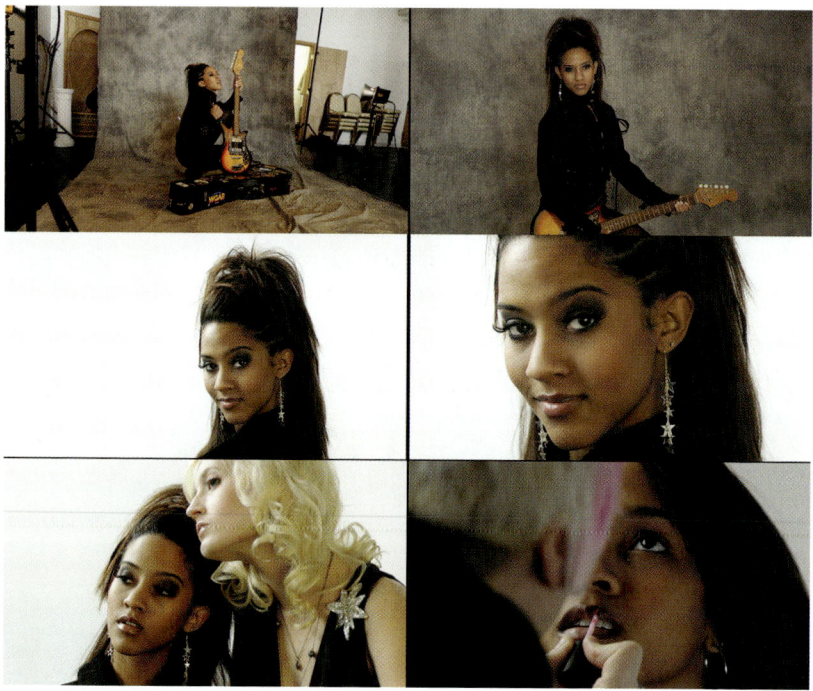

Figure 6.8 Establishing shot (top left), medium shot (top right), close-up (middle left), extreme close-up (middle right), two shot (bottom left), over-the-shoulder shot (bottom right).

Lighting for Video

Much like in still photography, how you handle light pretty much can make or break your videography. You can significantly improve the quality of your video by increasing the light falling in the scene. An inexpensive shoe mount video light, which will easily fit in a camera bag, can be found for $15 or $20. You can even get a good-quality LED video light for less than $100. Work lights sold at many home improvement stores can also serve as video lights since you can set the camera's white balance to correct for any colorcasts. Much of the challenge depends upon whether you're just trying to add some fill light on your subject versus trying to boost the light on an entire scene. A small video light in the camera's hot shoe mount or on a flash bracket will do just fine for the former. It won't handle the latter.

Lighting can either be hard (direct) or soft (diffused). Hard light is good for showing detail, but can also be very harsh and unforgiving. "Softening" the light, but diffusing it somehow, say, with an umbrella or white cardboard reflector, can reduce the intensity of the light but make for a kinder, gentler light as well.

Tips for Better Audio

Since recording high-quality audio is such a challenge, it's a good idea to do everything possible to maximize recording quality. Here are some ideas for improving the quality of the audio your camera records:

- **Get the camera and its microphone close to the speaker.** The farther the microphone is from the audio source, the less effective it will be in picking up that sound.
- **Use an external microphone.** The D5500's microphone port accepts a stereo mini-plug from a standard external microphone, allowing you to achieve considerably higher audio quality for your movies than is possible with the camera's built-in microphones (which are disabled when an external mic is plugged in). You can also use a wireless external microphone like the Nikon ME-W1. An external microphone reduces the amount of camera-induced noise that is picked up and recorded on your audio track.
- **Hide the microphone.** Combine the first few tips by using an external mic, and getting it as close to your subject as possible. If you're capturing a single person, you can always use a lapel microphone. But if you want a single mic to capture sound from multiple sources, your best bet may be to hide it somewhere in the shot. Put it behind a vase, using duct tape to fasten the microphone and fix the mic cable out of sight (if you're not using a wireless microphone).

WIND NOISE REDUCTION

Always use the windscreen provided with an external microphone to reduce the effect of noise produced by even light breezes blowing over the microphone. Many mics include a low-cut filter to further reduce wind noise. However, these can also affect other sounds. External mics often have their own low-cut filter switch.

■ **Turn off any sound makers you can.** Little things like fans and air handling units aren't obvious to the human ear, but will be picked up by the microphone. Turn off any machinery or devices that you can plus make sure cell phones are set to silent mode. Also, do what you can to minimize sounds such as wind, radio, television, or people talking in the background.

■ **Consider recording audio separately.** Lip-syncing is probably beyond most of the people you're going to be shooting, but there's nothing that says you can't record narration separately and add it later. It's relatively easy if you learn how to use simple software video-editing programs like iMovie (for the Macintosh) or Windows Movie Maker (for Windows PCs). Any time the speaker is off-camera, you can work with separately recorded narration rather than recording the speaker on-camera. This can produce much cleaner sound.

Chapter 7

Shooting Tips

Here you'll find tips on settings to use for different kinds of shooting, including recommended settings for some Shooting and Custom Setting menu options. You can set up your camera to shoot the main type of scenes you work with, then use the charts that follow to make changes for other kinds of images. Most will set up their D5500 for my basic settings, and adjust from there. I'm listing only the menu entries which have options that I recommend changing; for the other entries in each menu, you can select your own settings as appropriate.

Shooting and Custom Setting Menu Recommendations

I'll list my Photo Shooting menu recommendations first. The Custom Setting menu recommendations are divided into the exact same categories but, of course, deal with different options. In the first table, the second column shows the default settings, as the D5500 comes from the factory.

Table 7.1 Shooting Menu Recommendations #1

Option	Camera Default	Basic Setting	Studio Flash	Portrait
Image Format/Quality	JPEG Normal	NEF(RAW)+JPEG Fine	NEF	NEF+JPEG Fine
Image Size	Large	Large	Large	Large
White Balance	Auto	Auto	Preset Manual	Auto
Set Picture Control	Standard	(Standard + Sharp 7)	Standard	(Neutral + Sharp −2)
Color Space	sRGB	Adobe RGB	Adobe RGB	Adobe RGB
Auto Distortion Control	Off	Off	Off	Off
Active D-Lighting	Off	Off	Off	Off
Long Exp. NR	Off	Off	Off	Off
High ISO NR	Normal	Low	Low	Low
ISO Sensitivity Settings				
> ISO Sensitivity	100	200	200	200
> ISO Sensitivity Auto Control	Off	On	Off	Off
> *Maximum Sensitivity*	3200	800	1600	1600
> *Minimum Shutter Speed*	1/30 s	1/60 s	1/60 s	1/60 s
Movie Settings				
> *Frame Size/Movie Quality*	1920 × 1080/24 fps, high quality	1920 × 1080/24 fps, high quality	1920 × 1080/24 fps, high quality	1920 × 1080/24 fps, high quality
> *Microphone*	Auto sensitivity (A)	Auto sensitivity (A)	Auto sensitivity (A)	Auto sensitivity (A)

Table 7.2 Shooting Menu Recommendations #2

Option	Long Exposure	Sports Indoors	Sports Outdoors	Landscape
Image Format/Quality	NEF	JPEG Fine	JPEG Fine	NEF+JPEG Fine
Image Size	Large	Large	Large	Large
White Balance	Auto	Auto	Auto	Auto
Set Picture Control	Standard	Standard	Standard	(Vivid + Sharp 5)
Color Space	Adobe RGB	Adobe RGB	Adobe RGB	Adobe RGB
Auto Distortion Control	Off	Off	Off	On
Active D-Lighting	Off	Off	Off	Off
Long Exp. NR	On	Off	Off	Off
High ISO NR	Low	Normal	Low	Low
ISO Sensitivity Settings				
> ISO Sensitivity	400	1600	400	200
> ISO Sensitivity Auto Control	Off	Off	Off	Off
> *Maximum Sensitivity*	1600	1600	1600	1600
> *Minimum Shutter Speed*	1/60 s	1/60 s	1/60 s	1/60 s
Movie Settings				
> Frame Size/Movie Quality	1920 × 1080/24 fps, high quality	1280 × 720/30 fps, normal quality	1280 × 720/30 fps, normal quality	1920 × 1080/24 fps, high quality
> Microphone	Auto sensitivity (A)	Auto sensitivity (A)	Auto sensitivity (A)	Auto sensitivity (A)

Table 7.3 Custom Setting Menu Recommendations #1

Item	Option	Camera Default	Basic Setting	Studio Flash	Portrait
Autofocus					
a1	AF-C priority selection	Focus	Focus	Release	Release
a2	Number of focus points	39	39	39	11
a3	Built-in AF-assist illuminator	On	On	Off	Off
a4	Rangefinder	Off	Off	Off	On
Exposure					
b1	EV steps for exposure control	1/3 step	1/3 step	1/3 step	1/3 step
Timers/AE Lock					
c1	Shutter-release button AE-L	Off	On	Off	Off
c2	Auto off timers	Normal	Custom	Custom	Custom
	> Playback/Menus	20 sec.	8 sec.	8 sec.	8 sec.
	> Image review	4 sec.	8 sec.	8 sec.	8 sec.
	> Live view	3 min.	10 min.	10 min.	10 min.
	> Standby timer	8 sec.	8 sec.	8 sec.	8 sec.
c3	Self-timer	Delay: 10 sec. No. of Shots: 1	Delay: 10 sec. No. of Shots: 1	Delay: 10 sec. No. of Shots: 1	Delay: 10 sec. No. of Shots: 1
c4	Remote on duration (ML-L3)	1 min.	1 min.	1 min.	5 min.

Table 7.3 Custom Setting Menu Recommendations #1 (continued)

Item	Option	Camera Default	Basic Setting	Studio Flash	Portrait
Shooting/display					
d1	Exposure delay mode	Off	Off	Off	Off
d2	File no. sequence	Off	On	On	On
d3	Viewfinder grid display	Off	Off	Off	Off
d4	Date stamp	Off	Off	Off	Off
Bracketing/Flash					
e1	Flash cntrl for built-in flash	TTL	TTL	TTL	TTL
e2	Auto bracketing set	AE	AE	AE	AE
Controls					
f1	Assign Fn button	ISO	ISO	ISO	ISO
f2	Assign AE-L/AF-L button	AE-AF lock	AE-AF lock	AE-AF lock	AE-AF lock
f3	Assign touch Fn	ISO	ISO	Viewfinder grid display	Focus-point selection
f4	Reverse dial rotation	No	No	No	No

Table 7.4 Custom Setting Menu Recommendations #2

Item	Option	Long Exposure	Sports Indoors	Sports Outdoors	Landscape
Autofocus					
a1	AF-C priority selection	Focus	Release	Release	Focus
a2	Number of focus points	11	11	11	11
a3	Built-in AF-assist illuminator	Off	Off	Off	Off
a4	Rangefinder	On	Off	Off	Off
Exposure					
b1	EV steps for exposure control	1/3 step	1/3 step	1/3 step	1/3 step
Timers/AE Lock					
c1	Shutter-release button AE-L	Off	Off	On	Off
c2	Auto off timers	Custom	Normal	Custom	Custom
	> Playback/Menus	20 sec.	20 sec.	8 sec.	8 sec.
	> Image review	10 sec.	8 sec.	20 sec.	8 sec.
	> Live view	10 min.	3 min.	10 min.	10 min.
	> Standby timer	8 sec.	8 sec.	8 sec.	20 sec.
c3	Self-timer	Delay: 10 sec. No. Shots: 1	Delay: 10 sec. No. of Shots: 1	Delay: 10 sec. No. of Shots: 1	Delay: 10 sec. No. of Shots: 2
c4	Remote on duration	1 min.	1 min.	1 min.	1 min.

Table 7.4 Custom Setting Menu Recommendations #2 (continued)

Item	Option	Long Exposure	Sports Indoors	Sports Outdoors	Landscape
Shooting/display					
d1	Exposure delay mode	On	Off	Off	On
d2	File no. sequence	On	On	On	On
d3	Viewfinder grid display	Off	Off	Off	On
d4	Print date	Off	Off	Off	Off
Bracketing/Flash					
e1	Flash cntrl for built-in flash	TTL	TTL	TTL	TTL
e2	Auto bracketing set	AE	AE	AE	ADL
Controls					
f1	Assign Fn button	ISO	ISO	ISO	BKT
f2	Assign AE-L/AF-L button	AE-AF lock	AF-ON	AF-ON	AE-AF lock
f3	Assign touch Fn	ISO	Focus-point selection	Focus-point selection	Viewfinder grid display
f4	Reverse dial rotation	No	No	No	No

Index

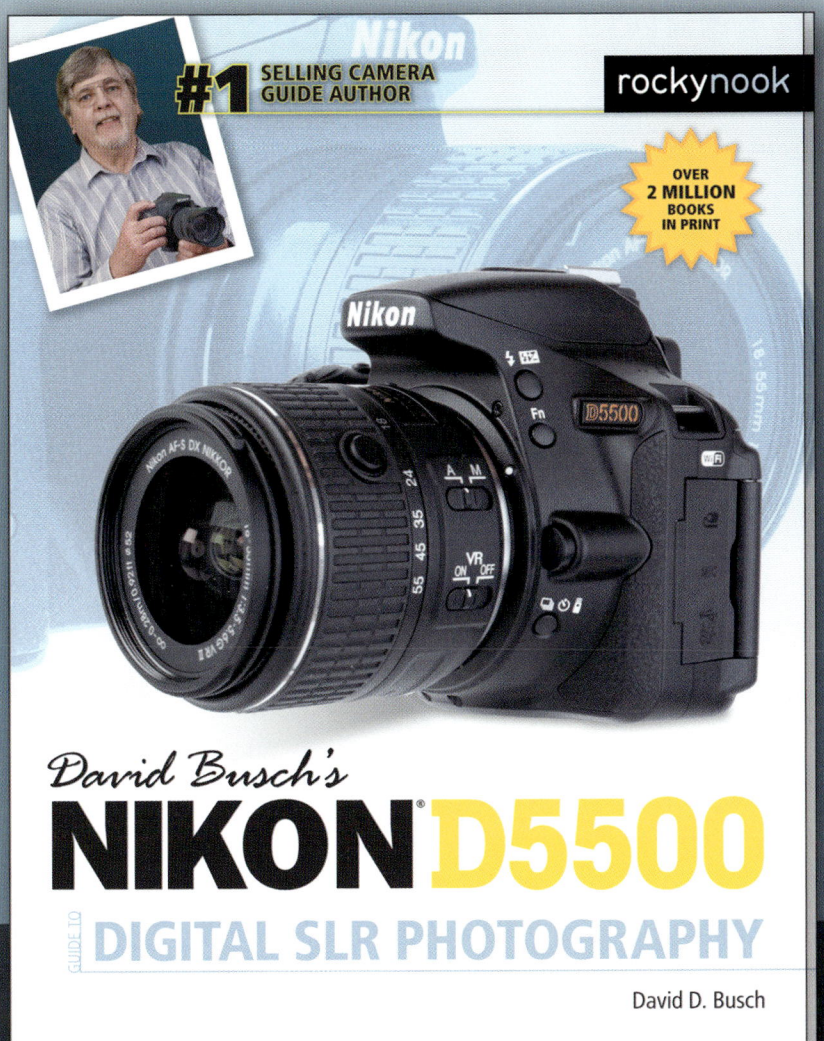